The

What, When and Where Guide

to Southern California

by
Basil Charles Wood

Doubleday & Company, Inc.
Garden City, New York

1979

To Doris, whose constant encouragement,
advice and sound practical help have made this book possible.
Without her, it just wouldn't exist.

Library of Congress Cataloging in Publication Data

Wood, Basil Charles.
The what, when, and where guide to southern California.

(A Dolphin book)
Includes index.
1. California, Southern—Description and travel—
Guide-books. I. Title.
F867.W7 1978   917.94'9'045
ISBN: 0-385-14043-6
Library of Congress Catalog Card Number: 78-3264

CONTENTS

How to use this guide____xi

Places to visit

AMUSEMENT PARKS

AREA NUMBER		PAGE NUMBER
37	Alpine Village	62
28	Busch Bird Sanctuary	52
37	California Alligator Farm	72
38	Disneyland	80
37	Knott's Berry Farm	76
28	Magic Mountain	50
37	Marineland of the Pacific	30
50	Sea World	16

ZOOS

38	Lion Country Safari	24
37	Los Angeles Children's Zoo	100
37	Los Angeles Zoo	100
50	San Diego Children's Zoo	2
50	San Diego Wild Animal Park	8
50	San Diego Zoological Gardens	2
26	Santa Barbara Zoological Gardens	36

TELEVISION STUDIOS (NETWORK)

AREA   PAGE

NUMBER   NUMBER

Area Number		Page Number
37	ABC Television Studios	74
37	CBS Television Studios	74
37	NBC Television Studios	74

ART GALLERIES

37	Huntington Library & Art Gallery	68
44	Irvine Bowl	22
44	Laguna Beach Museum of Art	22
49	La Jolla Museum of Contemporary Art	20
37	Long Beach Museum of Art	28
37	Los Angeles County Museum of Art	56
37	Los Angeles Municipal Art Gallery	54
37	Norton Simon Museum	64
50	San Diego Fine Arts Gallery	4
26	Santa Barbara Museum of Art	36
50	Spanish Village Arts and Crafts Center	8
50	Timken Art Gallery	8
37	UCLA Frederick S. Wight Art Gallery	58
37	Palos Verdes Art Center & Museum	82

MUSEUMS

50	Aerospace Museum	4
37	Beulah Hawkins Doll Museum	86
38	Briggs Cunningham Automotive Museum	78
40	Cabot's Old Indian Pueblo Museum	96
37	Cabrillo Marine Museum	28
50	California Museum of Science & Industry	106
27	California Oil Museum	42
38	Charles W. Bowers Memorial Museum	78
37	Citizens' Savings Athletic Foundation & Museum	60
11	Desert Museum	90

MUSEUMS

AREA NUMBER		PAGE NUMBER
39	Edward-Dean Museum of Decorative Arts	96
37	Ferndell Nature Museum	102
37	Fowler Museum	56
50	Hall of Champions	4
37	Hall of Science, Griffith Park	102
26	Historical Society Museum, Santa Barbara	36
37	Hollywood Wax Museum	54
9	Kern County Museum & Pioneer Village	48
39	Lincoln Shrine	98
37	Living Sea	26
37	Lomita Railroad	62
37	Los Angeles County Museum of Natural History	106
50	Maritime Museum Association	16
38	Movieland of the Air	78
37	Movieland Wax Museum	72
37	Movieworld	72
28	Museum of American Treasures	18
50	Museum of Man	6
26	Museum of Natural History, Santa Barbara	38
50	Natural History Museum, San Diego	6
50	Naval Training Center Museum	14
38	Orange Empire Trolley Museum	98
37	Pacificulture-Asia Museum	72
40	Palm Springs Desert Museum	94
37	J. Paul Getty Museum	86
29	Ventura County Historical Museum	34
30	Roy Rogers-Dale Evans Museum	92
39	San Jacinto Museum	96
16	San Luis Obispo County Historical Museum	40
49	Scripps Institution of Oceanography	20
36	Seabee Museum	34
50	Serra Museum Library & Tower Art Gallery	14
37	Southwest Museum	66
37	Travel Town	104

MISSIONS & PLACES OF WORSHIP

AREA NUMBER		PAGE NUMBER
50	Adobe Chapel	12
37	Forest Lawn Memorial Park, Glendale	54
37	Forest Lawn Memorial Park, Hollywood Hills	52
37	Los Angeles Mormon Temple	58
25	Mission La Purisima	40
27	Mission San Buenaventura	34
50	Mission San Diego de Alcala	18
28	Mission San Fernando Rey de España	50
37	Mission San Gabriel Arcangel	66
44	Mission San Juan Capistrano	22
16	Mission San Luis Obispo de Tolosa	40
44	Mission San Luis Rey de Francia	18
7	Mission San Miguel Arcangel	42
26	Mission Santa Barbara	34
25	Mission Santa Ines	40
37	Old Mission Church	110
37	Saint Sophia Cathedral	62
39	San Bernardino Asistencia	98
37	Wayfarers Chapel	30

STATE & COUNTY PARKS & HISTORIC LANDMARKS

38	Adobe de Palomares	82
37	Banning Mansion and Museum	62
50	Casa de Estudillo	10
50	Casa de Lopez	10
50	El Presidio Real de San Diego	14
37	El Pueblo de Los Angeles State Park	108
37	Exposition Park	106
18	Fort Tejon State Historic Park	48

STATE & COUNTY PARKS & HISTORIC LANDMARKS

AREA NUMBER		PAGE NUMBER
37	Griffith Park	100
6	Hearst San Simeon State Historical Monument	
25	La Purisima Mission State Historic Park	40
37	Los Encinos State Historic Park	50
37	Lummis El Alisal Home	66
38	Mission Inn	98
25	Mission La Purisima Concepcion	40
27	Mission San Buenaventura	34
50	Mission San Diego de Alcala	18
28	Mission San Fernando Rey de España	50
37	Mission San Gabriel Arcangel	66
44	Mission San Juan Capistrano	22
16	Mission San Luis Obispo de Tolosa	40
44	Mission San Luis Rey de Francia	18
37	Mission San Miguel Arcangel	42
26	Mission Santa Barbara	34
25	Mission Santa Ines	40
37	Old Plaza Fire House	110
50	Old Town San Diego	10
50	Old Town Drug Store	12
37	Old Spanish Plaza	110
37	Olvera Street	110
37	Pico House	110
37	Pio Pico State Historic Monument	70
23	Providence Mountains State Area	92
37	Rancho La Brea Tar Pits, George C. Page Museum	56
16	San Luis Obispo County Historical Museum	40
37	University of Southern California	106
50	Whaley House	12
28	William S. Hart Park	48
37	Will Rogers State Park	58

HOMES & BUILDINGS OF HISTORIC INTEREST

AREA NUMBER		PAGE NUMBER
37	Casa de Adobe	66
37	La Casa de la Centinela Adobe	60
37	La Casa de Rancho Los Cerritos	26
50	Derby Pendleton House	12
37	The Gamble House	62
36	Leonis Adobe	50
37	Rancho Los Alamitos	28
50	San Diego Union Office	10
26	Santa Barbara County Courthouse	36
1	Scotty's Castle	90
37	Towers of Simon Rodia	60

NATIONAL PARKS & MONUMENTS

50	Cabrillo National Monument	14
35	Channel Islands National Monument	42
1,2,4	Death Valley National Monument	88
40,41	Joshua Tree National Monument	92

BOTANICAL GARDENS & NATURE CENTERS

28	Descanso Gardens	64
37	El Dorado Nature Center	24
37	Los Angeles State & County Arboretum	70
37	Pierce College Nature Center and Farm	86
49	Quail Botanic Gardens	18
38	Rancho Santa Ana Botanic Gardens	82
50	San Diego Botanical Gardens and Building	4
26	Santa Barbara Botanic Garden	38
37	South Coast Botanic Gardens	32
38	Tucker Wildlife Sanctuary	78
37	UCLA Botanical Gardens	58
37	Whittier Narrows Nature Center	70

MISCELLANEOUS

AREA NUMBER		PAGE NUMBER
5	Amargosa Opera House	88
38	Arabian Horse Shows	82
50	Bazaar Del Mundo	12
19	Burton's Tropico Gold Mine	86
21	Calico Ghost Town	92
37	California Institute of Technology	64
37	Chinatown	104
37	Coliseum	106
26	Dos Pueblos Orchid Co.	38
37	Farmers Market	56
37	Fisherman's Village, Marina del Rey	32
37	Fisherman's Wharf, Redondo Beach	32
43	Glass Bottom Boat Trip	46
37	Greek Theatre	74
37	Griffith Observatory & Planetarium	102
37	Hollywood Bowl	52
37	Hollywood Park	60
50	House of Pacific Relations	6
49	La Jolla Caves	20
37	Lawry's California Center	48
37	Little Tokyo	104
37	Los Angeles City Hall	104
37	Los Angeles Civic Center	104
37	Los Angeles Memorial Sports Arena	106
37	Los Angeles Public Library	108
37	Los Angeles Swimming Stadium	106
37	Mann's Chinese Theater	54
37	Marineland Sky Tower	30
37	Mayfair Music Hall	32
6	Morro Bay Aquarium	42
37	Music Center for the Performing Arts	108
37	Occidental Center	108
50	Old Globe Theatre	6
40	Palm Canyon	94
40	Palm Springs Aerial Tramway	94
45	Palomar Observatory	96

MISCELLANEOUS

AREA NUMBER		PAGE NUMBER
37	Ports O'Call Village & Whaler's Wharf	28
37	Queen Mary	26
37	Rose Bowl	64
49	Salk Institute	20
50	San Diego Harbor Excursions	16
44	San Onofre Nuclear Information Center	22
37	Santa Anita Park	70
43	Santa Catalina Island	46
43	Scenic Terrace Drive	46
43	Seal Rookery Boat Trip	46
43	Skyline Drive	46
25	Solvang	38
50	Space Theater & Science Center	2
37	Universal Studios Tour	52

WINERIES

112

SCENIC CHAIR RIDES

84

INDUSTRIAL TOURS

114 to 122

HOW TO USE THIS GUIDE

If you have ever squinted through pages of small type to find out when a museum will be open, you will understand the reason for this guide. If you are a parent who has wrestled with an unwieldly road map in one hand and an oversized tourist book in the other, while the rest of the family cries, "How much farther?" you will find this guide a soothing antidote for travel headaches, eyestrain, heartburn and—perhaps best of all—an overextended budget.

This is a quick-reference guide, designed for everyone who wants to know at a glance WHAT there is to see . . . WHEN it's open . . . HOW MUCH it costs . . . and WHERE it can be reached by the simplest route.

How This Guide Can Save You Money

Use this guide in planning your trips by combining visits to several attractions that are all located in the same vicinity. Admission costs are clearly listed and many interesting places are free, so you can easily determine the amount you wish to spend and how far you want to travel without danger of getting lost or going over the top of your budget.

Southern California is a great, sprawling area, renowned for its comfortably warm climate and filled with so many interesting places to visit that if you don't know exactly where they are, it's easy to drive within a mile or so of one and miss it. This book has individual maps specially designed to accompany each subject, and also to show the location of other attractions close by, thereby sparing you unnecessary travel and saving costly gas.

For example, if you plan to visit Magic Mountain amusement park and you travel by freeway from Los Angeles, you will pass within half a mile of Busch Gardens and also the Mission San Fernando Rey de Espana, and the freeway exits for both places are clearly marked on the map. When you are at Magic Mountain you are also within five miles of the William S. Hart Park, and the accompanying map shows you how to get there. Only the principal roads; no unnecessary detail.

Tips on How to Use the Guide

The Table of Contents groups all attractions under major headings—Amusement Parks, Zoos, Museums, etc. If you would like to explore the Danish village of Solvang, for example, you will find it listed under "Miscellaneous Attractions." To the *left* will be a column headed "Area Number" and in that column opposite Solvang is the number 25. Now turn to the Area Map in the very front of this guide and you will see it is divided by a grid into numbered areas. This enables you to locate any attraction in relation to the whole of Southern California. Solvang is in area 25, which is well to the north of Los Angeles.

Opposite Solvang in the Table of Contents on the *right* hand side is a page number, in this case 38. Turn to page 38 and you will find Solvang described and a clear map showing how to get there. En route you may want to visit the Dos Pueblos Orchid Company and in Solvang there is also the Mission Santa Inez. The same page gives a detailed map of Santa Barbara and the location of several interesting places to visit in that city, together with everything you may want to know about opening hours, cost of admission and how to get there.

Industrial Tours

An added feature of this book is its listing of various industrial tours. It's fun to see how the things we use every day are made, operated, grown or packaged—and educational too. Many companies offer tours of their facilities and a selected list is included, beginning on p. 114. Not all tours are of interest to young children. Some companies specify age limits and also limit the number of persons per tour. Nearly all require reservations, so please be sure to telephone or write first (numbers and addresses are given in the Industrial Tour section).

The Guide as Your Traveling Companion

Your WHAT, WHEN AND WHERE GUIDE TO SOUTH-ERN CALIFORNIA packs a great deal into its 144 pages, but of course cannot be all-inclusive. It is not a restaurant guide, for instance; there are plenty of those. It does not include all state parks or historic monuments but concentrates on places of widest general interest located within the parks.

Opening and closing times may be affected by national or state holidays, and it is usually advisable to telephone before planning a visit on a holiday. Daylight saving changes may also cause an adjustment in the hours of operation. The hours listed were in effect when we went to press, as were the costs of admission.

Frequently used, kept around the house or in the glove compartment of your car, this guide will greatly stimulate and expedite your enjoyment of one of the world's most richly varied playgounds. All information has been checked against data supplied by the attraction managements, for which we are grateful, and it is my hope that you will find this book to be enormously useful as you explore the wonders of Southern California.

—Basil Charles Wood

SOUTHERN CALIFORNIA

AREA MAP

Each attraction in this guide has an Area Number shown on its accompanying map. The corresponding numbered square on this page shows its approximate location in Southern California.

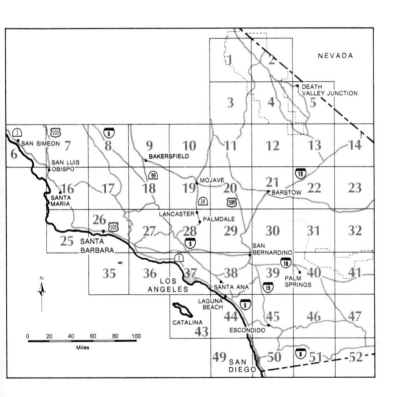

SAN DIEGO ZOOLOGICAL GARDENS

Balboa Park
San Diego
(714) 234-5151

Main Zoo

One of the largest zoos in the world. Among its great collection of animals are included some of the rarest specimens in captivity. Open-moated enclosures display such animals as elephants, giraffes, lions and tigers without bars or fencing.

A free-flight bird cage 90 feet high and 17 feet long is one of the largest in the world. A unique new attraction is the Skyfari aerial tramway which gives visitors an overall view of the extensive grounds and the animals.

A ride that is both informative and fun is the Guided Bus Tour, covering most of the Zoo's canyons and mesas. The driver-guide will introduce you to an exotic variety of Zoo-dwellers during the three-mile safari tour.

Children's Zoo

Set aside from the main zoo, the Children's Zoo is a miniature world designed and scaled for children. Baby animals may be petted and fed in a special enclosure. Displays include an incubator and hatchery for baby chicks, barnyard, walk-through bird displays, tortoise ride, seal pool and rodent tunnel.

Reuben H. Fleet SPACE THEATER & SCIENCE CENTER

Balboa Park
San Diego
(714) 238-1233

See Omnimax films and space-oriented multi-media shows projected on America's largest planetarium/theater screen—76 feet in diameter and inclined 25 degrees to the horizontal. Double features shown every day. Adults $2.75; Juniors (5–15): $1.50. Call 238-1168 for show times. (Includes admission to Science Center)

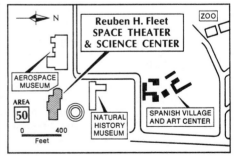

SAN DIEGO ZOOLOGICAL GARDENS

Richmond St

Zoo Dr

Richmond St Exit

Laurel Dr

El Prado

BALBOA

Park Blvd

395

163

PARK

Pershing Dr

5

Broadway

N

AREA 50

0   ¼
Mile

CHILDREN'S ZOO
Daily,
Same as Main Zoo

Over 16 25¢
Under 16 15¢

Science Center:
Daily, 10 am to 5 pm and
7 pm to 9:30 pm

Adults: 50¢
Juniors: (5–15) 25¢
Under 5 free

Free admission with purchase
of Space Theater ticket.)

N

**Reuben H. Fleet
SPACE THEATER
& SCIENCE CENTER**

ZOO

AEROSPACE
MUSEUM

AREA 50

0   400
Feet

NATURAL
HISTORY
MUSEUM

SPANISH VILLAGE
AND ART CENTER

3

AEROSPACE MUSEUM Balboa Park **San Diego** (714) 234-8291	Interesting and educational exhibits trace San Diego's important role in the development of aviation . . . past, present and future. Displays span the years from 1883 to today's Space Age. Close by is the Reuben H. Fleet Space Theater and Science Center where outstanding productions are presented daily. The Science Center is full of exhibits that are explorable, understandable and fun.
BOTANICAL GARDENS & BUILDING Balboa Park **San Diego**	Over 800 varieties of plants may be found in this beautiful botanical garden. At the north end is a reassembled Santa Fe Railroad station in which an interesting collection of tropical and sub-tropical plants is displayed. At the eastern end of El Prado is the beautiful Plaza de Balboa fountain, between the Space Theater and the Natural History Museum.
FINE ARTS GALLERY Balboa Park **San Diego** (714) 232-7931	An excellent collection of old masters is maintained as a permanent display, including Renaissance, Baroque, 18th-century Dutch, Flemish, Spanish and Italian paintings. There are also about thirty changing exhibitions held during the year. The Timken Art Gallery and Home of the Putnam Foundation Art Collection is adjacent to the Fine Arts Gallery.
HALL OF CHAMPIONS Balboa Park **San Diego** (714) 234-2544	Portraits, photographs and mementos are on display honoring many famous San Diego athletes in this sports museum, one of three similar foundations in the United States. A very wide range of athletic endeavor is represented in the Hall of Champions, covering amateur, college and professional sports.

WHEN TO GO AND WHERE TO FIND IT

Daily,
10 am to 4:30 pm

Free

Daily, except Fri.
10 am to 4:30 pm

Free

Daily,
Tues. through Sun.
10 am to 5 pm
Closed Mon.

Free

Daily,
Mon. through Sat.
10 am to 5 pm
Sun. 12 noon to 5 pm

Free

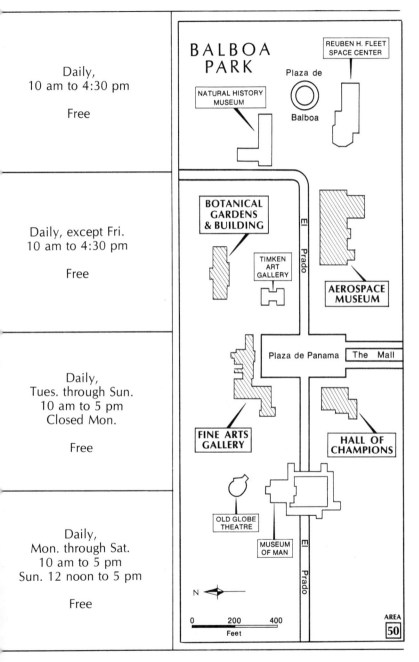

BALBOA PARK

REUBEN H. FLEET SPACE CENTER

Plaza de Balboa

NATURAL HISTORY MUSEUM

BOTANICAL GARDENS & BUILDING

El Prado

TIMKEN ART GALLERY

AEROSPACE MUSEUM

Plaza de Panama   The Mall

FINE ARTS GALLERY

HALL OF CHAMPIONS

OLD GLOBE THEATRE

MUSEUM OF MAN

El Prado

N

0   200   400
Feet

AREA
50

HOUSE OF PACIFIC RELATIONS Balboa Park, Palisades Area **San Diego** (714) 237-0739	This group of 15 cottages represents countries bordering on the Pacific Ocean. During summer months, weekly programs of folksongs, dances and talks about individual countries and their customs are given on the patio. A different cottage presents its own program every Sunday.
MUSEUM OF MAN Balboa Park **San Diego** (714) 239-2001	The story of mankind is depicted in this museum, where the permanent exhibit, "Wonder of Life," presents a view of how we all began. Exhibits are changed throughout the year and feature arts, crafts and antiquities, frequently dating back to man's earliest years on this planet. A fascinating glimpse of prehistoric man and his struggle for survival.
NATURAL HISTORY MUSEUM Balboa Park **San Diego** (714) 232-9146	Interesting displays may be seen in this museum which explore and interpret the nature of San Diego. Exhibits include birds, mammals, plants, insects, minerals, marine life and other components of the area. Programs of nature films are shown on Saturdays at 3 pm and Sundays at 1:30 pm and 3 pm.
OLD GLOBE THEATRE Balboa Park **San Diego** (714) 239-2255	An intimate, colorful playhouse with only 420 seats in a replica of Shakespeare's original 16-century Globe Playhouse. A professional acting company in rotating repertory is featured during the summer in the Shakespeare Festival. During winter months the theatre presents drama with professional actors, covering a wide range of subjects.

Open House
Sun. 2 pm to 5 pm,
April through Oct.

Free

Daily,
10 am to 4:45 pm

Adults: 75¢
Students with ID 35¢
Children: 6–15 10¢
Under 6 free

(Free admission Wed.)

Daily,
10 am to 5 pm

Adults: $1.00
Tues. free

Daily,
except Mon. 8 pm

Weekend matinees only, 2 pm

Adults: Weekends $3.50 &
$3.00
Weeknights $3.00 & $2.50
Children: 16 & under $2.00

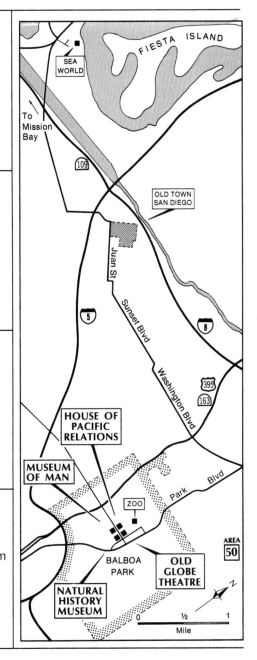

SPANISH VILLAGE ARTS & CRAFTS CENTER Balboa Park **San Diego** (714) 233-9050	In a setting of Spanish architecture, 41 commercial art and photography studios offer an interesting variety of crafts to the visitor. On weekends demonstrations are given by many artisans—painters, sculptors, potters, gold and silver craftsmen and weavers. Visitors are welcome to the open house, held daily.
TIMKEN ART GALLERY Balboa Park **San Diego** (714) 239-5548	The gallery is the permanent home for the Putnam Foundation Art Collection, featuring old masters, Italian Renaissance, Low Countries, Spanish and French works. There is also a large collection of Russian and Eastern Mediterranean icons. The Fine Arts Gallery, adjacent to the Timken Gallery, contains many old masters and holds numerous changing exhibitions.
SAN DIEGO WILD ANIMAL PARK State Route 78, 2 miles east of **Escondido** (714) 234-6541	A 1,800-acre wildlife preserve and authentic African-style village. Elephants, rhinos, lions, giraffes, zebras and many other creatures roam freely, separated from their natural enemies (and the public) by moats. A five mile train ride takes visitors to the five major exhibit areas. Nairobi Village is a 15-acre complex of exhibits, shows and shops. The Giant Aviary has a towering free-flight cage where more than 200 exotic birds live in a lush African setting. At the Elephant Wash visitors can watch young Asian elephants splashing in a large lagoon and at the Animal Care Center baby animals will be seen in their glass enclosures. Other exciting exhibits include the Giant Gorilla Grotto, the lively Toucan Gazebo and the exotic Water Fowl Lagoon.

Daily,
11 am to 4 pm

Free

Daily, except Mon.
Tues. through Sat.
10 am to 4:20 pm
Sun. 1:30 pm to 4:20 pm

Closed
during the month of August

Free

May 27 through Labor Day
9 am to 9 pm

Post-Labor Day through Oct.
and March through May 26:
9 am to 5 pm

Nov. through Feb.
9 am to 4 pm

Adults: $4.95
Under 16: $2.50
Under 6: free

Admission includes
all shows and exhibits.

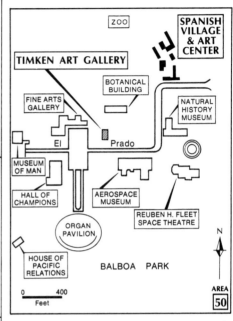

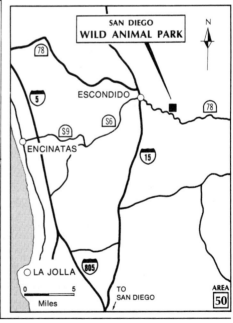

OLD TOWN SAN DIEGO HISTORIC State Park Visitor Center 4016 Wallace St. **San Diego** (714) 294-5182	The park is located in the central section of Old San Diego. In addition to many historical points of interest, the park contains shops, restaurants and other attractions that reflect the flavor of the Old Town historical period of 1821–72. Old Town San Diego was officially declared a State Historic Park in 1968 and buildings are being restored as they were a century ago.
CASA DE ESTUDILLO 2656 San Diego Ave. **San Diego** (714) 294-5182	This restored adobe contains many Spanish and early American authenic furnishings and relics. It was built in the late 1820s by Jose Antonio de Estudillo, grandson of a captain in the Spanish army. He married Maria Victoria Dominquez and their five sons and two daughters were born in the adobe. Estudillo was appointed Treasurer and Assessor of San Diego County when the American government was established.
CASA de LOPEZ 3890 Twiggs St. **San Diego** (714) 298-5352	The Casa de Lopez was constructed in the early 1830s and is one of the older buildings in this area of San Diego. It is now a candle shop and museum, and displays gifts and items from many nations. Free tours conducted daily.
SAN DIEGO UNION OFFICE (Casa de Altamirano) 2626 San Diego Ave. **San Diego** (714) 297-2119	This old wood frame building was the first home of the San Diego Union and has been restored as closely as possible to its appearance in 1868, when the first edition of the newspaper came off the press. The old press, trays of type, cookstove, lamps and an old calendar wall clock look as they did in San Diego's early days.

Daily
Summer 10 am to 6 pm
Winter 10 am to 5 pm

La Casa de Estudillo
and Seeley Stable 75¢

Rest of park free

Daily,
Summer 10 am to 6 pm
Winter 10 am to 5 pm

Adults: 50¢
Under 18 free

Daily,
9 am to 9 pm

Free

Daily, except Mon.
9 am to 5 pm

Free

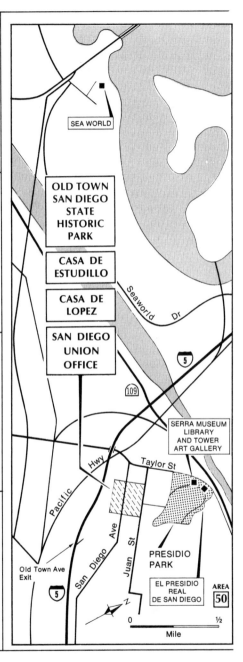

SEA WORLD

OLD TOWN
SAN DIEGO
STATE
HISTORIC
PARK

CASA DE
ESTUDILLO

CASA DE
LOPEZ

SAN DIEGO
UNION
OFFICE

Seaworld   Dr

5

109

SERRA MUSEUM
LIBRARY
AND TOWER
ART GALLERY

Hwy   Taylor St

Pacific

San Diego Ave

Juan St

PRESIDIO
PARK

Old Town Ave
Exit

5

EL PRESIDIO
REAL
DE SAN DIEGO

AREA
50

N

0   ½
Mile

11

ADOBE CHAPEL 3965 Conde St. **San Diego**	The original adobe chapel was dedicated in 1858, eight years after construction was begun, and has since been restored. The characters on which authoress Helen Hunt Jackson based her famous story *Ramona* were married here, and Father Antonio D Ubach, "Father Gaspara" of *Ramona*, officiated at the chapel.
WHALEY HOUSE AND OLD TOWN DRUG STORE 2482 San Diego Ave. **San Diego** (714) 298-2482	The first brick house to be built in San Diego, Whaley House was once a family residence and social center of the Old Town. Now fully restored, it serves as a museum offering many interesting historical items and fine period furniture. Also on the grounds of Whaley House is the Old Town Drug Store and Apothecary.
DERBY PENDLETON HOUSE 4017 Harvey St. **San Diego** (714) 298-2482	This unique house was once a home in New England. In 1851 it was shipped to California by way of Cape Horn, and then reassembled on its present site. It is now a museum and contains much of the original furniture. The museum is entered through Whaley House.
BAZAAR DEL MUNDO Old Town San Diego State Historic Park **San Diego** (714) 296-3161	Located in the famous Spanish Colonial Casa de Pico, this unusual group of small quality shops surrounds an attractive inner courtyard, garden, bandstand and native birds. Entertainment on the weekends. Visitors can purchase a wide assortment of Mexican food, folk arts, handmade jewelry, flowers, candles, books, furnishings, clothes, toys and paintings.

Sat. & Sun.
11:30 am to 1:30 pm

Free

Daily, except Mon. & Tues.
10 am to 4:30 pm

Adults: $1.25
Children: 12–16 60¢
5–11 30¢

Daily, except Mon. & Tues.
10 am to 4:30 pm

Adults: 50¢
Children: 12–16 25¢
Under 12 10¢

Daily,
Mon. through Sat.
10 am to 9:30 pm
Sun. 10 am to 5:30 pm

Free

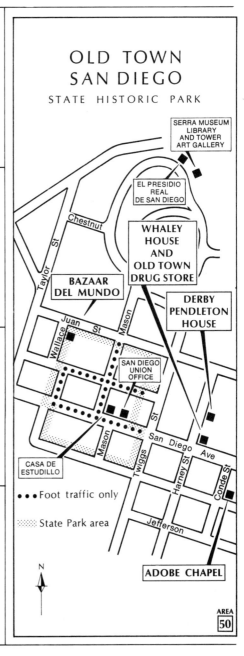

OLD TOWN
SAN DIEGO
STATE HISTORIC PARK

SERRA MUSEUM
LIBRARY
AND TOWER
ART GALLERY

EL PRESIDIO
REAL
DE SAN DIEGO

WHALEY
HOUSE
AND
OLD TOWN
DRUG STORE

BAZAAR
DEL MUNDO

DERBY
PENDLETON
HOUSE

Chestnut

Taylor St

Juan St

Wallace

SAN DIEGO
UNION
OFFICE

Mason

St

San Diego Ave

CASA DE
ESTUDILLO

Mason

Twiggs

Harney St

Conde St

●●● Foot traffic only

State Park area

Jefferson

N

ADOBE CHAPEL

AREA
50

13

SERRA MUSEUM LIBRARY & TOWER ART GALLERY 2727 Presidio Dr. **San Diego** (714) 297-3258	An impressive structure of Spanish Colonial architecture, the museum stands on a hill in Presidio Park, marking the location where Father Junipero Serra founded the first mission in Upper California. Displays depict the history of San Diego from 1562 to the present day.
EL PRESIDIO REAL de SAN DIEGO Presidio Dr. **San Diego** (714) 297-3258	The first white settlement in California and also the first mission and fort were located on this hill. The Presidio was the walled city built around the mission, but today only grassy mounds mark the site of these historical buildings. The officers' quarters and the barracks are roughly outlined by fallen walls.
CABRILLO NATIONAL MONUMENT Point Loma **San Diego** (714) 293-5450	This national monument, with an imposing statue of Juan Rodriguez Cabrillo, commemorates the discovery of the California coast in 1542. The "Old Lighthouse" built in 1854 is also part of the scene. In the new auditorium at the Visitors Center, hourly programs of slides and films are presented daily.
NAVAL TRAINING CENTER MUSEUM U.S. Naval Training Center **San Diego** (714) 225-5495	Maritime history is depicted in this large collection of ship models, paintings, photographs, historic Naval gear, old cannons and other memorabilia. NAVY OPEN HOUSE held aboard naval vessels from 1 pm to 4 pm Sat. and Sun. at the Broadway Pier. For current information telephone 235-3534. (Sat. and Sun. 235-3547). **Note:** *Enter at Gate 3, Point Loma*

Daily,
9 am to 5 pm

Free

Daily, except Mon.
10 am to 5 pm

Free

Daily,
9 am to 5:15 pm

Free

Daily,
Mon. through Fri.
8 am to 4 pm

Sat. and Sun.
1 pm to 4 pm

Free

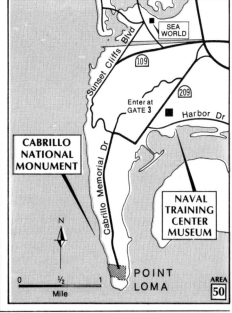

EL PRESIDIO REAL
DE SAN DIEGO

Taylor St

109

SERRA MUSEUM
LIBRARY &
TOWER
ART GALLERY

OLD TOWN
SAN DIEGO

Old Town Ave
Exit

San Diego Ave

5

N

Pacific Hwy

0   ½
Mile

AREA 50

SEA
WORLD

Sunset Cliffs Blvd

109

209

Enter at
GATE 3

Harbor Dr

CABRILLO
NATIONAL
MONUMENT

Cabrillo Memorial Dr

NAVAL
TRAINING
CENTER
MUSEUM

N

0   ½   1
Mile

POINT
LOMA

AREA 50

HARBOR EXCURSION Foot of Broadway and Harbor Dr. **San Diego** (714) 234-4111	A most interesting tour of San Diego Bay with such attractions as the U.S. Coast Guard Base, U.S. Naval and Marine Training Centers and the Mothball Fleet. *Two-hour cruises (Winter) 10 am and 2 pm (Summer) 10 am, 2 pm, 3 pm* *One-hour cruises (Winter) 11 am, 1 pm, 2:45 pm, 4:15 pm; (Summer) 10:30 am, 11:15 am, 12:15 pm, 1 pm, 1:45 pm, 2:30 pm, 3:15 pm, 4 pm, 4:45 pm, 5:30 pm.*
MARITIME MUSEUM ASSOCIATION 1306 N. Harbor Dr. **San Diego** (714) 234-9153	Located at the foot of Ash Street, the *Star of India* is a fine square-rigged iron sailing vessel built on the Isle of Man in England in 1863. Now joined by two other vessels, the ferryboat *Berkeley* and the steam yacht *Medea*, the "fleet" of the Maritime Museum Association presents an interesting panorama of maritime and naval history.
SEA WORLD 1720 South Shore Road Mission Bay **San Diego** (714) 222-6363	On the shores of Mission Bay, Sea World provides hours of family fun, instruction and entertainment with six continuous shows and many marine life exhibits and exciting water specialty acts. Performing dolphins, seals, sea lions and a killer whale are featured in an underwater theater. A two-acre Japanese Village in a beautifully landscaped park features daily exhibitions of pearl diving by the traditional Ama girls. Hydrofoil boat rides across the Bay, skytower rides and demonstrations of free flight kiting add to the fun. For the young children the California Tide Pool is both educational and exciting.

WHEN TO GO AND WHERE TO FIND IT

Daily.
hour cruise: Adults: $4.50
Children: 5–11 $2.25
Under 5 free

hour cruise: Adults: $2.75
Children: 5–11 $1.40
Under 5 free

Daily,
9 am to 8 pm

Adults: $2.00
Servicemen 50¢
Children: Under 12 50¢
Under 5 free

amily groups: $5.00 max.

Daily,
Summer: 9 am to dusk
Winter: 10 am to dusk

Adults: $5.95
Children: 4–12 $3.75
Under 4 free

One price admission
includes all shows
and exhibits

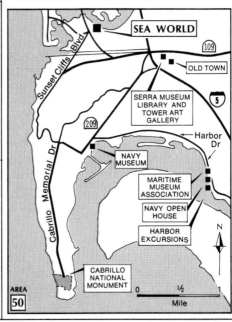

QUAIL BOTANIC GARDENS 230 Quail Gardens Dr. **Encinatas** (714) 436-3036	Twenty-six acres of gardens are open to th public at this pleasant spot in Encinata where the mild coastal climate is ideal for th growth of a great range of beautiful and rar plants. Self-guided trails are threaded through th grounds and a natural bird refuge and sanc tuary formed by an area of chaparral pro vides an opportunity to see a wide variety o resident and migratory fowl.
MISSION SAN LUIS REY de FRANCIA State Route 76 **Oceanside** (4 miles east) (714) 757-3651	Eighteenth in the chain of missions, this mag nificent structure was founded in 1798 b Padre Lasuén and named for King Louis IX o France. This is one of the largest of the missions with lofty beamed ceilings and original deco rations by the Indians of the area. At th height of its prosperity almost 3,000 Indian converts dwelt within its walls.
MISSION de SAN DIEGO de ALCALA Mission Valley Friars Rd. **San Diego** (714) 281-8449	First of a long line of missions to be built i upper California, San Diego de Alcalá wa originally established on Presidio Hill b Father Serra, but shortly afterwards rebuilt i Mission Valley where growing number could be accommodated. Often called the Mother Mission, it wa rebuilt in 1780 after destruction by the Indi ans and restored in 1941.
MUSEUM OF AMERICAN TREASURES 1315 East 4th Street **National City** (714) 477-7489	This unique museum contains an unusua collection of ivory carvings, bronzes, marble busts and a variety of artillery shell art. Other interesting artifacts on displa include Indian relics, cannon and other his torical pieces. There is also an exceptionally fine and large collection of American sun colored glass.

Daily, Summer:
8 am to 6 pm
Winter:
8 am to 5 pm

Free

Daily,
9 am to 4 pm

Self-guided tours:
Adults: 50¢
Children: Over 12 25¢

Daily,
9 am to 5 pm

Adults: 50¢
Children: under 12 free

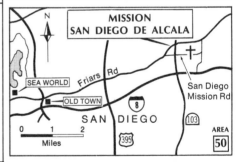

Sun. 10 am to dusk

Free
Donation appreciated

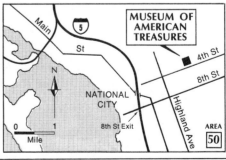

19

SALK INSTITUTE FOR BIOLOGICAL STUDIES 10010 N. Torrey Pines Rd. **La Jolla** (714) 453-4100	One of the world's largest independent centers of biological research. The smallest element of life, the cell, and its interaction with other cells and the environment is one of the Institute's major concerns. Better understanding of this interaction will provide answers to our many serious scientific and medical challenges: cancer, diabetes, growth and development defects, immunology, and the brain and nervous system.
SCRIPPS INSTITUTION OF OCEAN-OGRAPHY 8602 La Jolla Shores Dr. **La Jolla**	As the oceanographic branch of the University of California, San Diego, the center has earned a worldwide reputation for its research and graduate training in the fields of marine science. The Thomas Wayland Vaughan Aquarium-Museum features many fascinating marine specimens from around the globe.
LA JOLLA MUSEUM OF CONTEMPORARY ART 700 Prospect St. **La Jolla** (714) 454-0183	Housing a permanent collection of approximately 3,000 works of art, this fine museum provides an opportunity to today's best artists to display their talents and enable the public to see and experience current trends in the visual arts. Important new works are added to the permanent collection each year.
LA JOLLA CAVES and Curio Shop 1325 Coast Blvd. **La Jolla** (714) 454-6080	The largest of seven ocean-carved caves can be reached through a long tunnel, descending with 133 steps from the Cave Store at the top of the cliffs. The man-made tunnel is well lighted and the steps are easy to negotiate. Fossilized shells show that the sea has been boring into the rock and sandstone here for more than 200,000 years.

Every Wed. 2 pm
Public lecture, slide show
and tour.
Program lasts approx.
one hour

Free

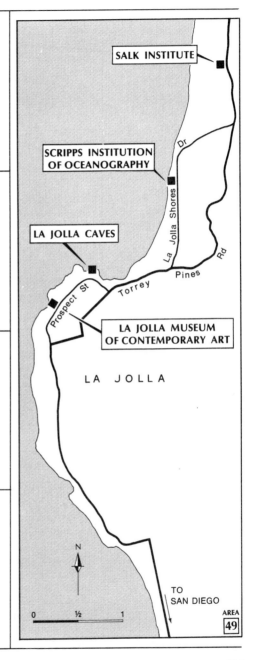

Daily:
9 am to 5 pm

Free

Daily, except Mon.

Tues. through Fri.
10 am to 5 pm

Sat. & Sun.
12:30 pm to 5 pm

Wed. 7 pm to 10 pm

Free

Daily, June through Sept.
10:30 am to 5 pm

Closed Wed.
during winter months

Adults: 50¢
Children: 2 to 11 25¢
Under 2 free

21

IRVINE BOWL 650 Laguna Canyon Rd. **Laguna Beach** (714) 494-1145	The annual Festival of Arts at Laguna Beach encompasses many displays by local residents. Highlight of the Festival is the Pageant of the Masters (nightly, 8:30 pm, adm. $5.00 to $10.00—a re-creation of great works of painting and sculpture, posed by living models and presented in a beautiful outdoor setting.
LAGUNA BEACH MUSEUM OF ART 307 Cliff Dr **Laguna Beach** (714) 494-6531	The Laguna Beach Museum of Art, a designated cultural site of Orange County, has a proud history dating back to 1918. There is a frequent change of exhibits, sponsor home tours, antique shows, bus trip and lecture series. The museum shop offers an excellent selection of books, jewelry and interesting artifacts.
MISSION SAN JUAN CAPISTRANO Camino Capistrano and Ortega hwy. **San Juan Capistrano** (714) 493-1111	Possibly the grandest and most beautiful of all the missions. Today the main church lies in ruins, but Padre Serra's Church, an adobe structure on the east side of the patio, was restored and is used daily for Mass. The legend of the punctual swallows is closely woven into the history of the mission. The birds arrive every March 19, St. Joseph's Day, and leave October 23.
SAN ONOFRE NUCLEAR INFORMATION CENTER Basilone Rd. **San Clemente** (714) 492-5272	Overlooking the site of the San Onofre Nuclear Generating Station, the information center contains many interesting displays and self-operated exhibits explaining the conversion of the atom to its use in the generation of electricity. A film which shows the uses of nuclear energy can also be seen.

22

WHEN TO GO AND WHERE TO FIND IT

July 15 to Aug. 28
noon to 11:30 pm

Outdoor arts and
crafts display

Adults: 50¢
Children: 6–12 10¢
Under 5 free

Daily,
11:30 am to 4:30 pm

Free

Daily,
7 am to 5 pm

Self-guided tours:
Adults: 50¢
Children: Under 12 free

Daily,
9 am to 4:45 pm

Free

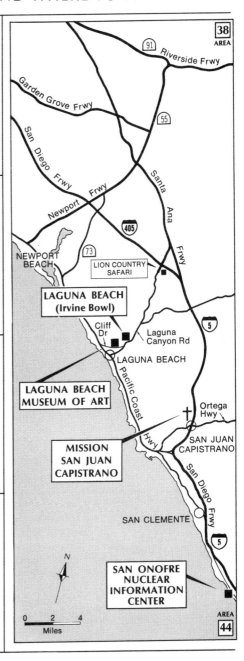

LION COUNTRY SAFARI

Moulton Parkway
Laguna Hills

(714) 837-1200

Free-roaming wild animals on a 500-acre game preserve is the unique concept of this fascinating "big-game park." Visitors drive their cars along an eight-mile trail where wild animals occasionally nuzzle up to the car for closer examination of their human "caged" visitors!

A pride of lions may casually stroll across the trail—all animals have right of way—and many others will approach for a closer look. The animals are well-fed, but are wild and unpredictable. Car windows must be rolled up almost tight. Convertibles are not permitted but air-conditioned cars may be rented. Pets are prohibited; free kennels are available.

There is an African Village, a boat ride through a lagoon where hippopotamuses, monkeys and water fowl can be seen and, for young children, a special compound where they can pet very tame baby animals. There are also bird shows, a puppet theatre, films and other attractions.

EL DORADO NATURE CENTER

7550
East Spring St.
Long Beach

(213) 425-8569

This 80-acre semi-wilderness situated in the center of a busy metropolitan area contains two lakes, hiking trails, a stream and a nature center building.

Trails have well-marked points for identification of flora and fauna and the nature center houses displays and photographs of plant-life and animals. Red fox, raccoon, weasel, and other mammals inhabit the area.

Daily, 9 am

Last car admitted:
Summer, 6 pm
Spring and Fall, 5 pm
Winter, 3:30 pm

Adults: $4.95
Children 3–11 $2.95
Under 3 free

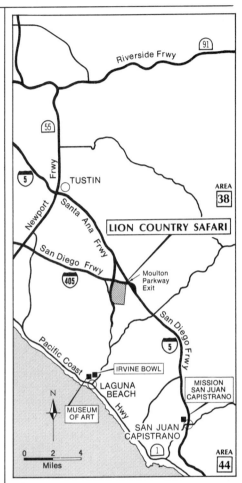

Daily, except Mon.

July through Aug.
9 am to 4 pm

Sept. through June
ues. Thurs. Fri. 2 pm to 4 pm
Wed. Sat. Sun. 9 am to 4 pm

Free

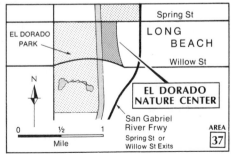

25

QUEEN MARY

Pier J
Long Beach

(213) 435-4733

Once the largest and swiftest ocean liner, the Queen Mary is now permanently moored at pier J at the southern end of the Long Beach Freeway. There is an unusual bus service every 30 minutes from downtown Long Beach via red doubledecker English buses.

The tour of the ship encompasses all 12 decks where visitors may explore the bridge, upper decks, luxurious staterooms, officers' quarters, and the engine rooms with their 26-inch-thick propeller shafts.

The Living Sea

Mid-point of the tour is *The Living Sea*, a marine museum created by the famous oceanographer, explorer and scientist, Jacques Cousteau. An undersea city of tomorrow, a futuristic undersea farm and unusual sea creatures form part of the world's largest marine exhibition, currently consisting of 10 major displays. It is located amidships, above and below the waterline.

Visitors will also enjoy the many specialty shops and restaurants, ranging from magnificent banquet rooms to fast-food facilities.

La CASA de RANCHO LOS CERRITOS

4600
Virginia Road
Long Beach

(213) 424-9423

One of the finest restored houses in California, the ranch house was built in 1844. Adobe bricks for the walls were made on the grounds. The redwood beams came from the forests near Monterey and many of the original beams still remain.

The ranch house is an historical museum and reference library furnished in the period of the late 1800's.

Summer:
Daily, 10 am to 4:30 pm.

Winter:
Mon. through Fri.
10 am to 3:30 pm

Weekends and holidays
10 am to 4:30 pm

Adults: $5.00
Children: 5–11 $1.75
Under 5 free

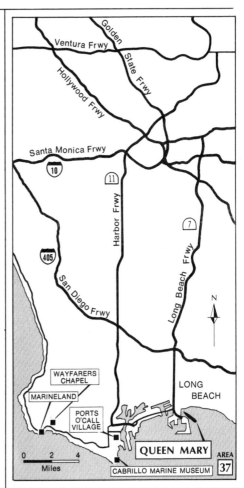

Daily, except Mon. & Tues.
1 pm to 5 pm

Free

27

WHAT TO SEE AND WHAT TO DO

CABRILLO MARINE MUSEUM 3720 Stephen White Dr. **San Pedro** (213) 831-3207	More than 15,000 foreign and local sea shells form the extensive collection in the museum, which also houses more than 100 varieties of Southern California fish, including the tiny grunion, a pigmy sperm whale and a 400-pound sunfish. An 1100-pound Leatherback turtle, lobsters, jellyfish and a giant 10-foot long deep water Japanese crab are also prominently displayed.
PORTS O'CALL VILLAGE and WHALER'S WHARF Berth 77 **San Pedro** (213) 831-0287	A distillation of the world's romantic seaports from Marseilles to Singapore, the 70 shops of the Village give visitors a taste of the places called on by merchant shipping. Whaler's Wharf simulates a 19th-century New England seaport, complete with cobbled streets.
LONG BEACH MUSEUM OF ART 2300 East Ocean Blvd. **Long Beach** (213) 439-2119	In an elegant brick and lava stone mansion, built in 1912 on a site overlooking the Pacific, American art of the twentieth century forms the permanent collection of this museum. Of particular interest is work created during the revolutionary activity of the New York school.
RANCHO LOS ALAMITOS 6400 Bixby Hill Rd. **Long Beach** (213) 431-2511	Rancho Los Alamitos is one of the oldest adobe structures still in use in California. Built in 1806 from the clay-like adobe soil, hand-patted and dried in the sun, the building has walls four feet thick. Today this splendidly furnished rancho, standing in beautifully landscaped grounds, is a graceful reminder of early California days.

Daily,
9 am to 5 pm
Sun. 12–4 pm

Free

Daily,
11 am to 9 pm

Free

Daily, except Mon., Tues.
12 noon to 5 pm

Free

Daily, except Mon. & Tues.
1 pm to 5 pm

Free

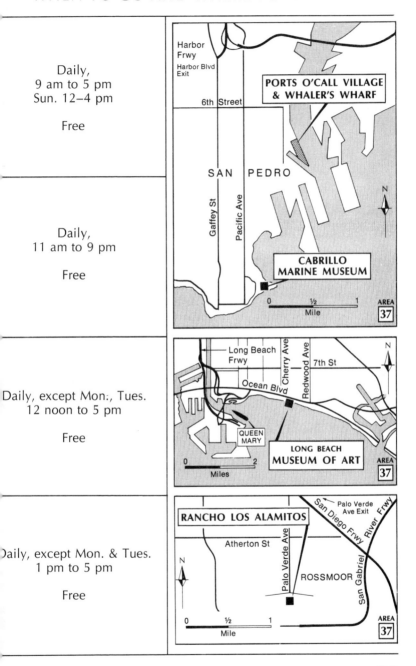

Harbor Frwy

Harbor Blvd Exit

6th Street

PORTS O'CALL VILLAGE & WHALER'S WHARF

SAN PEDRO

Gaffey St

Pacific Ave

N

CABRILLO MARINE MUSEUM

0   ½   1
Mile

AREA
37

Long Beach Frwy

Cherry Ave

Redwood Ave

7th St

N

Ocean Blvd

QUEEN MARY

LONG BEACH MUSEUM OF ART

0   2
Miles

AREA
37

RANCHO LOS ALAMITOS

San Diego Frwy

Palo Verde Ave Exit

San Gabriel River Frwy

Atherton St

Palo Verde Ave

N

ROSSMOOR

0   ½   1
Mile

AREA
37

MARINELAND OF THE PACIFIC Palos Verdes Drive, South **Palos Verdes Hills** (213) 489-2400	Come share the Marineland Experience. New for this season is the Family Adventure Swim—a first for any theme park; selected volunteer guests will swim among 400 fishes in a half-million-gallon tank, all facilities and equipment provided. At Sea Lion Point guests can relax and observe a rare colony of Sea Lions in their natural environment. The new Touch Tanks allow visitors to touch and examine fascinating sea creatures including sea anemones, starfish, sea urchins and more. Performing killer whales, dolphins, pilot whales and sea lions star in regularly scheduled shows. Other attractions include Pirate's Cove playground for the youngsters, pearl diving, penguin pool and flamingo exhibit, otters, aquariums displaying a variety of exotic fish etc. Snack bar and gift shop facilities.
MARINELAND SKY TOWER Located inside Marineland	This glass enclosed two-level elevator revolves slowly as it carries passengers high above Marineland. From the top you will have breathtaking views of the coastland, the Palos Verdes Peninsula and, on a clear day, Catalina Island. The ride takes four minutes to lift passengers 344 feet above sea level.
WAYFARERS CHAPEL Palos Verdes Drive, South **Portuguese Bend**	This very unusual and beautiful chapel was designed by Lloyd Wright, son of the famous architect Frank Lloyd Wright. Constructed of redwood, stone and glass, it is surmounted by a 50-foot tower which is a noted landmark from both land and sea. The church is of the Swedenborgian denomination.

Daily,
10 am to 5 pm

Mid-April to Mid-June,
10 am to 6 pm

Rest of Summer,
10 am to 7 pm

Adults: $5.50
Children 4–11 $3.75
Children under 4 free

Daily,
Included in admission

Daily,
11 am to 4 pm

Sun. service 11 am

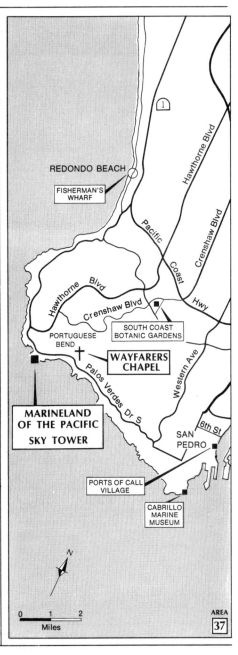

REDONDO BEACH

FISHERMAN'S WHARF

Hawthorne Blvd

Crenshaw Blvd

Pacific Coast Hwy

Hawthorne Blvd

Crenshaw Blvd

PORTUGUESE BEND

SOUTH COAST BOTANIC GARDENS

WAYFARERS CHAPEL

Western Ave

Palos Verdes Dr S

MARINELAND OF THE PACIFIC SKY TOWER

SAN PEDRO

6th St

PORTS OF CALL VILLAGE

CABRILLO MARINE MUSEUM

N

0   1   2
Miles

AREA
37

31

MAYFAIR MUSIC HALL 214 Santa Monica Blvd. **Santa Monica** (213) 451-0621	This theater offers a bright musical melang of British-style music hall where the aud ence is encouraged to join in and and sin along with the "Chairman" just as in th "old days." Programs change frequently and detai can be found in the entertainment section c the newspapers. There is also a restaurar within the theater.
FISHERMAN'S VILLAGE **Marina del Rey** (213) 823-5411	Waterside restaurants . . . unusual shops . . souvenir stores . . . sport fishing . . . boa rental . . . Fisherman's Village has somethin; of interest for everyone. The Village Boathouse has bait, tackle an rents sail and power boats. Thirty-minut harbor cruises are given on the *Marina Belle*
FISHERMAN'S WHARF Monstad Pier **Redondo Beach** (213) 372-2111	The Pier at Redondo Beach has unusua shops and restaurants, fresh fish stalls and souvenir stores. During summer month many restaurants stay open until 2 am. Redondo Sport Fishing Co. offers 45-min harbor cruises, leaving on the hour, 10 am t 5 pm (summer months only). For fisherman bait and tackle are available for rent.
SOUTH COAST BOTANIC GARDENS 26701 Rolling Hills Rd. **Palos Verdes Peninsula** (213) 772-5813	The South Coast Botanic Garden rests on trash dump! Three feet of topsoil coverin; over 3 million tons of trash have transformec this 87-acre site into a delightful garden witl walkways, waterfalls, a small lake and more than 150,000 plants. Tram tours carry visitors through the gar dens, where there are trees, plants and shrubs from Africa, Mexico, Australia and South America.

32

WHEN TO GO AND WHERE TO FIND IT

...eck newspaper listings for programs and times.

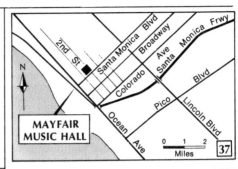

Daily,
...hops open during summer ...m 10 am to approx. 11 pm. Close earlier in winter.

Marina Belle Cruises:
Adults: $1.25
Children 6–12 50¢
Under 6 free

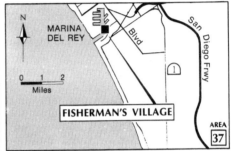

All Year

Shops and restaurants:
Daily, 11 am to 9 pm
(Later in summer)

Harbor cruises:
Adults: $1.00
Children under 12: 50¢.

Daily,
9 am to 5 pm

Free

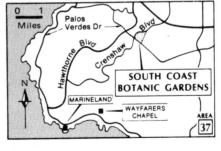

MISSION SANTA BARBARA Upper Laguna St. **Santa Barbara** (805) 966-3153	The great stone church of Satna Barbar known as the "Queen of the Missions" is or of the best preserved structures and a favori subject for photographers. Many relics of the mission days can l seen in the curio room, chapel and librar The mission is still in daily use as a paris church.
MISSION SAN BUENA-VENTURA 211 E. Main St. **Ventura** (805) 643-4318	This was the ninth and last mission founde by Father Junípero Serra, who died two yea later, on August 28, 1784. The church suffered heavy damage durir the earthquakes of 1812–13. Final restora tion of the buildings to their original appea ance was completed in 1976. The missio was noted for its fine grazing lands an gardens.
CEC/SEABEE MUSEUM Code 2232, Bldg. 99, Naval Construction Battalion Center **Port Hueneme** (805) 982-5163	The museum was established in 1947 at th Naval Construction Battalion Center, Po Hueneme, as a lasting monument to th fighting spirit of the Civil Engineer Corp "Seabees" during World War II. Displays include the history and memora bilia of the Seabees and there is a wide var ety of souvenir items which can be pu chased by visitors.
VENTURA COUNTY HISTORICAL MUSEUM 100 E. Main St, **Ventura** (805) 648-6131 Ext. 2701	A visit to this museum recalls the early day of California. The exhibits represent muc local history and provide a picture of life an industry in the area as it was many years agc On display are artifacts from thos pioneering days, including objects of Span ish, Mexican and Indian origin. Other inte esting exhibits include a number of shi models.

Daily,
9 am to 4:45 pm
Sun 1 pm to 4:45 pm

Self-guided tours:
Adults: 50¢
Children: Under 16 free

Daily,
10 am to 4 pm

50¢ donation

Daily,
Mon. through Fri.
8 am to 4:30 pm

Sat. 9 am to 4:30 pm
Sun. 12:30 pm to 4:30 pm

Free

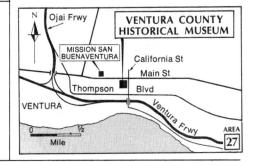

Daily, except Sun.
Mon. through Fri.
9 am to 4:30 pm
Sat. 12:30 to 4 pm

Free

SANTA BARBARA MUSEUM OF ART 1130 State St. **Santa Barbara** (805) 963-4364	Exhibits in this museum cover a spectrum ranging from American and European art to Oriental, Greek and Roman antiques. Film and slide lectures are given; special art classes are available for children and young people. The museum shop has art objects, jewelry and other items suitable for personal use or as gifts.
SANTA BARBARA COUNTY COURTHOUSE 1120 Anacapa St. **Santa Barbara** (805) 965-3021	A graceful Spanish-Moorish structure surrounded by lawns and tropical gardens. The elegant interior has hand-painted ceilings, wrought iron chandeliers, giant historical murals and many exhibits. Visitors will enjoy the sweeping view of the ocean from the clock tower.
HISTORICAL SOCIETY MUSEUM 136 East De La Guerra **Santa Barbara** (805) 966-1601	This small museum contains many treasures of the town's historic past. One wing is devoted to the Mexican and Spanish era, while other areas cover the American period and mementos of Santa Barbara's Chinese colony. The museum is the home of the Santa Barbara Historical Society.
SANTA BARBARA ZOOLOGICAL GARDENS 1300 E. Cabrillo Blvd. **Santa Barbara** (805) 962-5339	Covering 81 acres, the Santa Barbara Zoological Gardens contain many interesting attractions including a zoo, sealarium, bird refuge, western playground, Child's Estate and a miniature train which encircles the grounds. There is a charge of 50 cents for the miniature train ride. Children under 3 free.

Daily, except Mon.
11 am to 5 pm
Sun: noon to 5 pm

Free

Daily,
Mon. through Fri.
8 am to 5 pm

Sat. & Sun. 9 am to 5 pm

Free

Daily, except Mon.
12 noon to 5 pm

Sat. and Sun.
1 pm to 5 pm

Donation

Daily, except Mon.
10 am to 5 pm

Adults: $1.25
Children: 13–18 75¢
2–12 50¢
Under 2 free

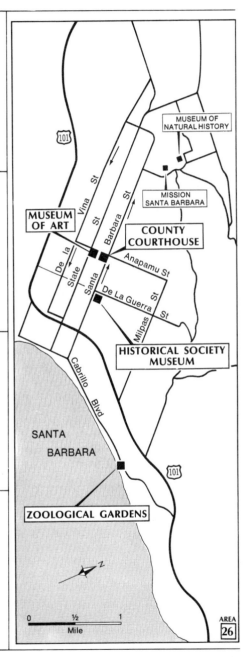

MUSEUM OF
NATURAL HISTORY

MISSION
SANTA BARBARA

MUSEUM
OF ART

COUNTY
COURTHOUSE

Vina St

Barbara St

De la

State

Santa

Anapamu St

De La Guerra St

Milpas St

HISTORICAL SOCIETY
MUSEUM

Cabrillo Blvd

SANTA

BARBARA

ZOOLOGICAL GARDENS

N

0   ½   1
Mile

AREA
26

SOLVANG **(Little Denmark)** Northwest of **Santa Barbara**	This very unusual community is a center for the Danish population. Many shops feature Scandinavian handicrafts and the town is famous for its enticing bakeries, serving pastries and coffee. The town has a Danish church, school and college. A large windmill and thatched roofs lend enchantment to the Old World atmosphere.
DOS PUEBLOS **ORCHID** **COMPANY** **Goleta** (805) 968-3535	One of the country's greatest collections of cymbidium and cattleya orchids is maintained at the Dos Pueblos Orchid Company. In the display house an immense profusion of colors awaits the visitor. The company is on part of the historic 4,500-acre Rancho Dos Pueblos. March, April and May are the best months to enjoy a visit when the blooms are at their finest.
SANTA **BARBARA** **BOTANIC** **GARDEN** 1212 Mission Canyon Rd. **Santa Barbara** (805) 963-1886	Established in 1926, the garden now covers 70 acres, offering visitors the opportunity to wander leisurely through delightful areas of trees, flowering shrubs, cacti and flowers. There are trails to follow, with excellent literature to assist in identification of the varying plants, shrubs, birds and insects.
MUSEUM OF **NATURAL** **HISTORY** 2559 Puesta del Sol Rd. **Santa Barbara** (805) 963-7821	Principally dealing with the natural phenomena of the West, the museum contains well-executed exhibits, many of which are interesting and understandable to young children. There is also a Planetarium on the grounds, open to the public on the 1st and 3rd Monday of the month at 3 pm, and the 2nd and 4th Thursday at 8 pm.

Daily,
most shops are
open by midmorning,
close promptly at 5 pm

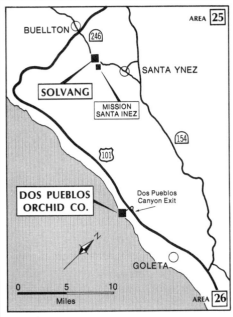

Daily,
9 am to 4 pm
except holidays

Free

Daily,
8 am to sunset

Closed during rainy weather

Free

Daily,
Mon. through Sat.
9 am to 5 pm
Sun. 10 am to 5 pm

Free

SAN LUIS OBISPO COUNTY HISTORICAL MUSEUM 696 Monterey St. **San Luis Obispo** (805) 543-0638	The museum contains many historical papers, portraits, glassware and Indian artifacts relating to the area and, since 1956, has occupied a building that was originally the city's Carnegie Library, constructed in 1905. The Cigar Factory, built in 1897, was formerly an active Victorian factory operation. It can be reached from the museum by foot bridge, crossing the San Luis Creek.
MISSION SAN LUIS OBISPO DE TOLOSA Chorro and Palm Sts. **San Luis Obispo** (805) 543-6850	Founded by Father Sérra in 1772, the mission was developed into a fine adobe structure by priests who where aided by local Indians. This was one of the first missions to use tile for roofing, in order to resist flaming arrows from hostile Indian tribes. The buildings have been well restored and contain a museum of old photographs and relics.
LA PURISIMA MISSION State Historic Park Lompoc Casmalia Road **nr. Lompoc** (4 miles)	Eleventh in the chain of missions, La Purisíma Concepción was founded by Father Lasuén in 1788. Destroyed in the earthquake of 1812, the mission was rebuilt three years later. A small museum contains artifacts; mission crafts are often demonstrated during the summer months.
MISSION SANTA INES 1760 Mission Dr. **Solvang** (805) 688-4815	Mission Santa Ines was the 19th of the 21 missions that stretched from San Diego to San Francisco. Its setting in the beautiful valley of the Santa Ynez River contrasts sharply with its turbulent history. Known for its beautiful façade and an arcade of 21 graceful arches, the mission also has an interesting museum of artifacts and vestments.

40

Daily, except Mon.
10 am to 12 noon
1 pm to 4 pm

Free

Daily
Summer: 9 am to 5 pm
Winter: 9 am to 4 pm

Free

Daily,
9 am to 5 pm

Closed holidays

Adults: 50¢
Children: Under 18 free

Daily,
9 am to 5 pm

Self-guided tours:
Adults: 50¢
Children: Under 16 free

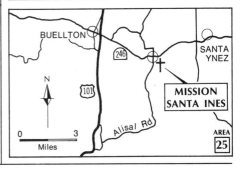

SAN LUIS OBISPO COUNTY HISTORICAL MUSEUM

MORRO BAY

SAN LUIS OBISPO

MISSION SAN LUIS OBISPO DE TOLOSA

N

0 2 4
Miles

AREA 16

VANDENBURG VILLAGE

LA PURISIMA MISSION STATE HISTORIC PARK

LOMPOC

BUELLTON

MISSION SANTA INES

SOLVANG

N

0 5
Miles

AREA 25

BUELLTON

SANTA YNEZ

MISSION SANTA INES

Alisal Rd

N

0 3
Miles

AREA 25

WHAT TO SEE AND WHAT TO DO

CHANNEL ISLANDS NATIONAL MONUMENT	These two islands form part of a chain of eight small islands once connected to the mainland. No services are available. Visitors must bring their own food, water and fuel. Camping is permitted but transportation must be arranged privately. **Note:** *For information and an excellent illustrated pamphlet, write: Superintendent, National Park Service, P.O. Box 1388, Oxnard, 93032. For transportation to the islands and tour information write: Island Packers, P.O. Box 993, Ventura, Cal. 93003.*
CALIFORNIA OIL MUSEUM 1003 Main St. **Santa Paula** (805) 525-4422	The history of oil in California, its discovery and the subsequent development of the industry is depicted in this museum. Many interesting and historical photographs are on display, together with a variety of exhibits including an early wooden drilling rig.
MISSION SAN MIGUEL ARCANGEL Highway 101 **San Miguel** (805) 467-3256	One of the most attractive of the missions, maintained in immaculate condition by the Franciscan Order. Today San Miguel Arcangel is a parish church and monastery. It contains outstanding examples of Spanish art in the form of murals, painted by Indians in 1823 under the direction of the artist Esteban Munras.
MORRO BAY AQUARIUM 595 Embarcadero **Morro Bay** (805) 772-7647	Sharks, seals, turtles, eels, octopuses, abalone, crabs, lobsters and fish of all sizes can be seen in this marine museum located on the waterfront. The aquarium is both engrossing and educational and provides a close-up look at many of the inhabitants of the Pacific Ocean. Children enjoy the opportunity to feed the seals.

Free

VENTURA
Ventura Frwy
101
1
N
SEABEE
MUSEUM
**CHANNEL ISLANDS
NATIONAL MONUMENT**
0   15
Miles
AREA
35

Daily,
except Mon. & Tues.
10 am to 4:30 pm

Free

**CALIFORNIA
OIL MUSEUM**
0   5   10
Miles
Frwy
VENTURA
126
SANTA
PAULA
Santa Paula
N
Ventura
101
Frwy
SEABEE
MUSEUM
OXNARD
PORT HUENEME
1
AREA
27

Daily,
10 am to 5 pm

Self-guided tours

Donation

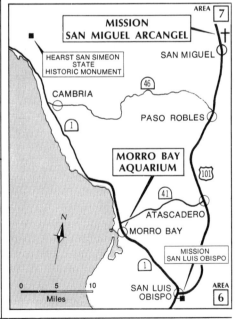

AREA 7
**MISSION
SAN MIGUEL ARCANGEL**
SAN MIGUEL
HEARST SAN SIMEON
STATE
HISTORIC MONUMENT
46
CAMBRIA
PASO ROBLES
1
**MORRO BAY
AQUARIUM**
101
41
ATASCADERO
N
MORRO BAY
MISSION
SAN LUIS OBISPO
1
0   5   10
Miles
SAN LUIS
OBISPO
AREA
6

Daily
Summer: 9 am to 8 pm

Winter: Mon. to Fri.
10 am to 5 pm
Weekends 9 am to 7 pm

Adults: 70¢
Children: 6–11 35¢
Under 6 free

HEARST SAN SIMEON
State Historical Monument
Off St. Rt. 1
San Simeon

San Simeon is a part of California's heritage, epitomizing a time in America when it was possible for one man to amass a private collection of priceless treasures and to build a home . . . a castle . . . of grandeur and magnificence wherein he could entertain like a king and provide a setting to match the opulence of his dreams. Such a man was William Randolph Hearst.

Today *La Casa Grande,* the 137-foot high Hispano-Moorish mansion, stands on the Enchanted Hill, a coastal knoll set against the Santa Lucia Mountains and aptly named by Hearst. It is surrounded by 123 acres of gardens, pools, terraces and palatial guest houses. The perfect setting for a "castle," although he never referred to it as such. To Hearst, it was always home.

He began building in 1922 and, at the time of his death in 1951, La Casa Grande was still unfinished, but by then had over 100 rooms including 38 bedrooms, 31 bathrooms, 14 sitting rooms, a movie theater and 2 libraries.

San Simeon is only open to the public through conducted tours, during which visitors will see much of the $50 million collection of art and antiques. Unlike the majority of museums and galleries, visitors cannot wander at will.

Details of the tours and how to make reservations and obtain tickets are given in the adjoining column.

he estate is open to visitors
iroughout the year, with the
xception of Thanksviving
id Dec. 25. Three tours are
fered, each covering spe-
fic areas of the house and
ounds. It is recommended
at Tour 1 be taken first.

Each tour lasts two hours.
omfortable walking shoes
iould be worn. Cars are
arked in a lot just off State
t. 1. Special buses transport
sitors to the castle grounds.

The cost of the tours:

Tour 1 Adults: $5.00
        Children: 6–18
        $2.00
        Under 6 free

Tour 2 Adults: $5.00
        Children: 6–18
        $2.00
        Under 6 free

Tour 3 Adults: $5.00
        Under 6 free

ickets are sold from 8 am
laily at the ticket booth. Visi-
ors should arrive early, as
ours are often sold out by
nidmorning. Tickets may
ilso be purchased through a
icketron outlet, or be
ibtained up to 60 days in
idvance by writing to: Ticke-
ron Inc., P.O. Box 26430,
ian Francisco, Calif. 94126.
here is an 80¢ per ticket reservation fee.

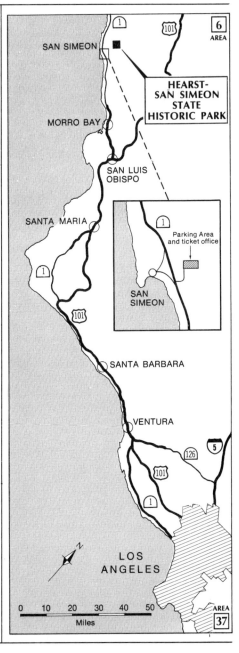

45

SANTA CATALINA
ISLAND

Lying 22 miles off the coast from Los Angeles, Catalina can easily be reached by boat or by air, with frequent daily departures. A visit to the island can be a very enjoyable one-day excursion, or you may stay overnight or longer at one of the motels or hotels in Avalon, the principal center of population.

This attractive island has a pier, fine beaches, a golf course and deep-sea fishing. There are several tours which give visitors an opportunity to enjoy many of the unusual features that Catalina has to offer, including:

Glass Bottom Boat Trip (40 min.): A fascinating view of strange marine life and colorful fish.

Scenic Terrace Drive (40 min.): Magnificent views high above the city and the bay during this scenic mountain drive.

Seal Rookery Boat Trip (40 min.): Watch the seals frolic and play along Catalina's rocky coastline.

Skyline Drive (1¾ hrs.): Outstanding views of Avalon and the mountains, with a stop at Catalina's "Airport in the Sky".

Other tours are available to visitors staying overnight or longer.

Catalina can be reached by boat from San Pedro or Long Beach. For departure times call or write to:

Long Beach/Catalina Cruises
Queen's Way Landing, 330 Golden Shores Blvd.
Long Beach 90802 (213) 775-2654

For flight information, call (213) 547-1161 or (213) 421-8281

ROUND-TRIP FARES:

From San Pedro

Adults: $10.00
Children: 5–11 $5.00
Under 5: 80¢

From Long Beach

Adults: $10.00
Children: 5–11 $5.00
Under 5: 80¢

Glass Bottom Boat Trip

Adults: $2.75
Children: 5–11 $1.50

Scenic Terrace Drive

Adults: $2.50
Children: 5–11 $1.25

Seal Rookery Boat Trip

Adults: $1.50
Children: 5–11 $1.00

Skyline Drive

Adults: $3.50
Children: 5–11 $2.00

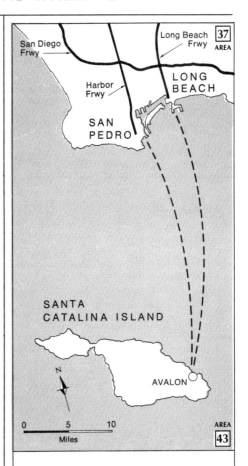

LONG BEACH/CATALINA CRUISES
Take Long Beach Freeway south to Downtown Long Beach exit. Go under Broadway sign, then ½ mile to Golden Shore exit.

CATALINA ISLAND CRUISES
Take Harbor Freeway south to Catalina Island exit. Terminal is located under the Vincent Thomas bridge.

WHAT TO SEE AND WHAT TO DO

KERN COUNTY MUSEUM AND PIONEER VILLAGE 3801 Chester Av. **Bakersfield** (805) 861-2132	Adjoining the museum, which houses many worthwhile exhibits of local origin, the Pioneer Village takes the visitor back into the late 19th century. Many old-time stores and buildings may be seen, including a drug store, doctor's office, firehouse, Kern County'sfirst courthouse, an old oil rig, locomotive, caboose, etc. Also on display: sixteen vintage horsedrawn vehicles, one of the finest collections of its kind in western America.
FORT TEJON State Historic Park, Highway 99 Nearest town **Lebec** (5 miles)	Fort Tejon is one of the outstanding historic parks in California. The fort was established by the United States Army on August 10, 1854, but abandoned ten years later. Now restored, the barracks building, officers' quarters and orderlies' quarters show the type of structures which were used.
LAWRY'S CALIFORNIA CENTER Ave. 26 at San Fernando Rd. **Los Angeles** (213) 225-2491	Discover this hideaway oasis just minutes from downtown Los Angeles where visitors seek and find escape from everyday city life. There's much to do. Dine informally in the beautiful gardens, visit and browse through gift and wine shops, and take a tour to see how Lawry's products are made.
WILLIAM S. HART COUNTY PARK 24151 Newhall Ave. **Newhall** (805) 259-0855	The famed movie star of the silent screen willed the ranch to Los Angeles County when he died in 1946. Visitors may now see memorabilia of his western movie days in the ranch house, while in the main house, completed in 1928, original furnishings and paintings by the noted western artist Charles M. Russell are on display. There is also a collection of famous firearms.

48

Daily, May 1 to Oct. 1

on. to Fri. 8 am to 3:30 pm
Sat. & Sun. 12 to 5:30 pm
Check with museum
for winter schedule

ioneer Village: Adults: 50¢
Children: 12–18 35¢
6–12 25¢ Under 6 free
Museum free

All year

Adults: 50¢
Children: Under 18 free

Daily, except Sun.
Lunch and shopping
11 am to 3 pm

uided tours: weekdays only

Admission and tours free

Museum:
Tues. through Sun.
10 am to 5 pm

Park:
Daily, 10 am
to one hour before sunset

Free

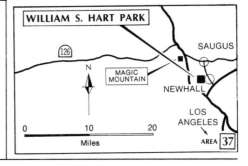

49

WHAT TO SEE AND WHAT TO DO

MAGIC MOUNTAIN Magic Mountain Pkwy. **Valencia** (805) 259-7272	Home of the Revolution, the world's large steel roller coaster, featuring the world's fir 360-degree vertical loop, *Magic Mountai* boasts over 50 "White-Knuckler" thrill ride and attractions, all for one admission pric There is a delightful "please touch" An mal Farm, a craft village and a wide varie of places to shop. On summer evenings th Showcase Theatre features some of the bi, gest names in the entertainment world.
MISSION SAN FERNANDO REY de ESPANA **Mission Hills** (213) 361-0186	This majestic mission was founded in 179 for travellers between the Gabriel and Sa Buenaventura missions. It also ministered the large Indian population of the Encin Valley. The church, major-domo's house, wor rooms and residence quarter have bee restored; other interesting features includ the underground wine vats, an Indian cra room and a museum.
THE LEONIS ADOBE 23537 Calabasas Rd. **Calabasas** (213) 346-3683	This is a restoration of an adobe ranch hous that was once the home of Miguel Leonis an his Indian wife, Espiritu. The adobe is furnished with original la 19th century furniture. There is also a bar containing artifacts, old wagons, a restore blacksmith forge and other interestin mementos.
LOS ENCINOS STATE HISTORIC PARK 16756 Moorpark St. **Encino** (213) 784-4849	The Franciscan padres used Encino as thei headquarters while exploring the valle before establishing Mission San Fernando i 1797. It was at the spring on this historic sit in 1769 that Gaspar de Portolá made a brie stop. Today the visitor can see the restored De l Osa Adobe in a fine state of preservation The nine-room house is of mission-type con struction with walls two feet thick.

Daily, Mem. Day to Labor
Day, 10 am to midnight
st of year Sat. Sun. & School
ol., Mid-Sept. to Oct., 10 am
o 10 pm. Nov. to Mem. Day,
10 am to 6 pm
Adults: $7.95
Children: 3–11 $6.95
Under 3 free

Daily, 9 am to 5 pm
Sun. 10 am to 5 pm

Self-guided tours
(last tour 4:15 pm)

ults: 75¢ Children: 7–15 25¢
Under 7 free

Wed. Sat. and Sun.
1 pm to 4 pm

Free
Donation requested

Tours:
Wed. through Sat.
1 pm to 4 pm
Sun. 1 pm to 5 pm

Adults: 50¢
Children: 6–17 25¢
Under 6 free

WHAT TO SEE AND WHAT TO DO

BUSCH BIRD SANCTUARY 16000 Roscoe Blvd. **Van Nuys** (213) 997-1171	The 21½-acre park includes a tropical boat cruise, trained-bird shows, animal exhibits, multi-media extravaganza, hospitality pavilions for sampling Anheuser-Busch products plus restaurants and shops. Guests can also take an enjoyable tour of the adjacent Anheuser-Busch Brewery aboard a unique monorail.
UNIVERSAL STUDIOS TOUR Hollywood Fwy. at Lankershim Blvd. **Universal City** (213) 877-1311	How movies are made and special effects created are features of this four and one-half hour, two-part tour. A narrated tram ride through many familiar exterior sets is followed by a stop at the Studio Entertainment Center. (No tours on Thanksgiving or Dec. 25)
FOREST LAWN MEMORIAL PARK, HOLLYWOOD HILLS Forest Lawn Drive **Hollywood** (213) 254-3131	Early America is recreated in the 15-acre Court of Liberty, featuring a 60-foot bronze and marble monument to Washington, Paul Revere's Old North Church, America's largest mosaic, "The Birth of Liberty," and a bronze by Saint-Gaudens of President Lincoln. **Note:** *Forest Lawn is a religious cemetery and place of worshop. Please dress accordingly.*
HOLLYWOOD BOWL 2301 N. Highland Ave. **Hollywood** (213) 876-8742	Set in a natural amphitheater in the Cahuenga Hills, the Hollywood Bowl is a gigantic open-air show place seating more than 17,000 persons. A series of summer concerts features the Los Angeles Philharmonic Orchestra. Other programs feature leading pop and jazz artists and, at Easter, the memorable Easter Sunrise Service.

52

Daily: 10 am to 6 pm
mid-June through Labor Day

Remainder of year
Wed. through Sun.

No admission charge
Parking: $1.00
Tropical Boat Cruise:
Adults: $1.00
Children: 50¢

Daily, 9 am to 5 pm
(mid-June to mid-Sept.)

Rest of year
10 am to 3:30 pm

Adults: $6.25
Children: 12–16 $5.25
5–11 $4.25
Under 5 free

Daily
8:30 to 5:30

Free

Daily,
9 am to 5 pm
mid-July through mid-Sept.

Call 87-MUSIC
for program information

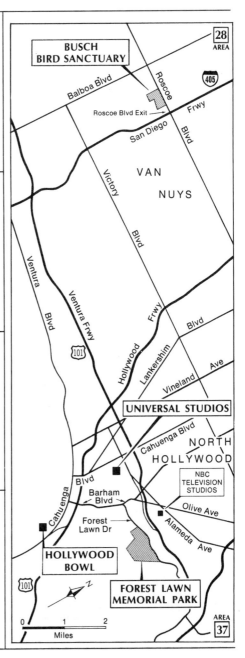

MANN'S CHINESE THEATER 6925 Hollywood Blvd. **Hollywood** (213) 464-8111	Constructed in the expansive days preceding Hollywood and filmdom's greatest era, this famous movie theater has impressions of the hands and feet of many of the most famous film personalities recorded for posterity in the concrete of the courtyard. The interior of the theater is lavishly decorated.
HOLLYWOOD WAX MUSEUM 6767 Hollywood Blvd. **Los Angeles** (213) 462-8860	Movie stars, presidents and historic personages are depicted here in lifesize wax figures. In the Chamber of Horrors monsters and murderers wait to greet you. Great moments in history include the Yalta Conference. Another major attraction is a faithful lifesize recreation of Leonardo da Vinci's "The Last Supper".
LOS ANGELES MUNICIPAL ART GALLERY Barnsdall Park 4800 Hollywood Blvd. **Los Angeles** (213) 660-2200	Traditional and contemporary art are displayed in this gallery located within Barnsdall Park. Exhibitions are frequently changed. Film series, musical presentations and other programs are also given. Call 660-2200 for ticket information and schedule of programs.
FOREST LAWN MEMORIAL PARK, GLENDALE 1712 South Glendale **Glendale** (213) 241-4151	The world's largest collection of original American bronze sculpture and statuary includes Frederick Remington's "Bronco Buster" and Gutzon Borglum's "The Dying Chief". Also on public display are an exact replica of Michelangelo's "La Pieta", Jan Styka's "The Last Supper" and a Leonardo da Vinci-inspired "Last Supper Window." **Note:** *Forest Lawn is a religious cemetery and place of worship. Please dress accordingly.*

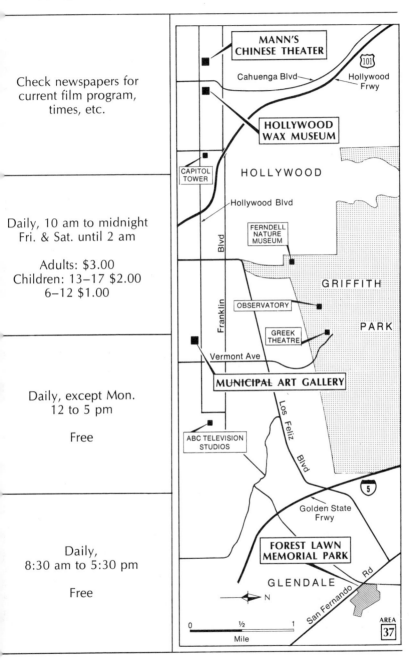

Check newspapers for current film program, times, etc.

Daily, 10 am to midnight
Fri. & Sat. until 2 am

Adults: $3.00
Children: 13–17 $2.00
6–12 $1.00

Daily, except Mon.
12 to 5 pm

Free

Daily,
8:30 am to 5:30 pm

Free

MANN'S
CHINESE THEATER

Cahuenga Blvd

Hollywood
Frwy

101

HOLLYWOOD
WAX MUSEUM

CAPITOL
TOWER

HOLLYWOOD

Hollywood Blvd

FERNDELL
NATURE
MUSEUM

Blvd

GRIFFITH

Franklin

OBSERVATORY

PARK

GREEK
THEATRE

Vermont Ave

MUNICIPAL ART GALLERY

Los Feliz Blvd

ABC TELEVISION
STUDIOS

5

Golden State
Frwy

FOREST LAWN
MEMORIAL PARK

San Fernando Rd

GLENDALE

N

0   ½   1

Mile

AREA
37

55

WHAT TO SEE AND WHAT TO DO

FOWLER FOUNDATION MUSEUM 9215 Wilshire Blvd. **Beverly Hills** (213) 278-8010	An outstanding collection of European and Asiatic decorative arts includes fine English silver, intricately carved ivories, rare and unusual firearms and ceramics. Many items in the museum have unique historical associations, such as the Rasputin Chalice, a personal gift to the mysterious court figure from Tsarina Aleksandra Fyodorovna.
LOS ANGELES COUNTY MUSEUM OF ART 5905 Wilshire Blvd. **Los Angeles** (213) 937-4250	A magnificent art museum housed in three gleaming pavilions surrounded by the B. G Cantor Sculpture Garden. The Ahmanson Gallery contains the permanent collections. The Frances and Armand Hammer Wing features special changing exhibitions and the Contemporary Art Galleries, and the Leo S Bing Center has a theater, educational facilities and an outdoor cafeteria.
RANCHO LA BREA TAR PITS, George C. Page Museum Hancock Park 5801 Wilshire Blvd. **Los Angeles** (213) 936-2230	Some 4,000 years ago many animals became trapped in the black, bubbling La Brea pits and the remains of mastodons, mammoths and other prehistoric creatures have been found preserved in the tar. Their skeletons are displayed in the County Museum of Natural History's branch, the George C. Page La Brea Discoveries Museum. See page 106 for information on the County Museum of Natural History.
FARMERS MARKET Third St. at Fairfax Ave. **Los Angeles** (213) 933-9211	During the depression, Farmers Market was a vacant lot on the edge of the city where farmers were allowed to sell their wasting crops. This original idea has developed over the years into a great market-giftshop-restaurant complex serving thousands of visitors and shoppers daily. In this unusual market you can eat lunch at an open-air restaurant.

Daily, except Sun.
1 pm to 5 pm

Free

Tues. to Fri. 10 am to 5 pm
Sat. 10 am to 6 pm
Sun. 10 am to 6 pm

Free

Recorded information:
tel. (213) 937-2590

Daily, except Mon.
10 am to 5 pm

Free

Daily, except Sun.

Summer: 9 am to 8 pm
Winter: 9 am to 6:30 pm

Free

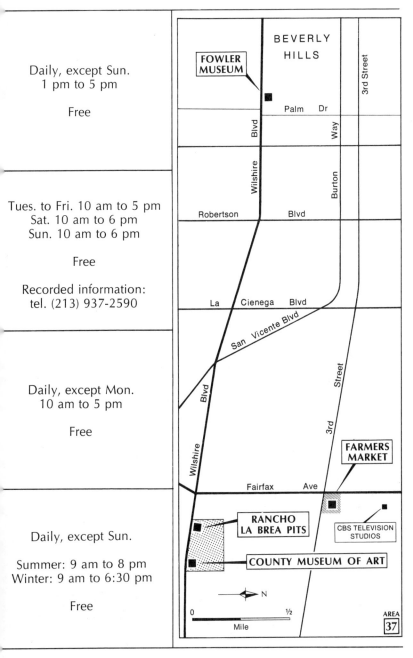

57

LOS ANGELES MORMON TEMPLE 10777 Santa Monica Blvd. **Los Angeles** (213) 474-1549	The world's largest Mormon temple is a noted West Los Angeles landmark, its striking white 257-foot tower topped by a 15-foot goldleafed statue of the Angel Moroni. At the Visitors Center guides conduct free tours where an outstanding variety of displays including movies and dioramas tell the story of the Mormons. Pictures of the interior of the Los Angeles Temple are also in evidence.
UNIVERSITY OF CALIFORNIA, LOS ANGELES 405 Hilgard Ave. Westwood **Los Angeles** (213) 825-4338	UCLA is the Los Angeles campus of the state-wide University of California, occupying a 411-acre site in Westwood. During the regular school year, conducted walking tours of the campus are given on the first Thursday of each month. On the following Thursdays, special tours feature the Frederick S. Wight Art Galleries, the Botanical Gardens and other places of interest. Tours start at 1:30 pm from the lobby of Schoenberg Hall, the music building. During the summer vacation the schedule is changed. Telephone the Visitor Center, 825-4338, for current information.
WILL ROGERS STATE HISTORIC PARK 14253 Sunset Blvd. **Pacific Palisades** (213) 454-6501	The ranch was presented to the State of California on August 19, 1944, after the death of Mrs. Rogers. The grounds and house are maintained as they were when the great humorist lived there with his family. Polo ponies are still kept in the stables and games are played throughout the year.

Daily, 9 am to 9 pm

Free

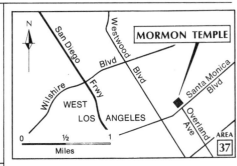

Conducted tours
of the campus each Thurs.,
at 1:30 pm.

Free

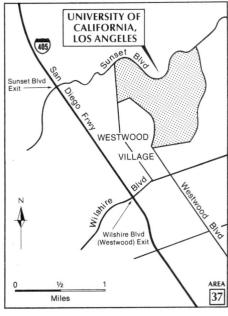

Daily,
8 am to 5 pm

Will Rogers House:
Daily, 10 am to 5 pm

Entrance fee
to Park and House
$1.50 per vehicle

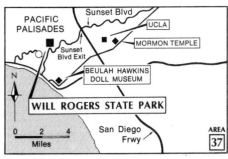

CITIZENS SAVINGS ATHLETIC FOUNDATION & MUSEUM 9800 S. Sepulveda Blvd. **Los Angeles** (213) 670-7550	An outstanding collection of sports trophie and athletic memorabilia may be seen in the Hall of Fame Athletic Museum. The names o those selected for inclusion in the Hall o Fame are drawn from an extensive range o athletic endeavor covering amateur, collage and professional sports.
CENTINELA ADOBE 7634 Midfield Ave. **Los Angeles** (213) 649-6272	The Centinela Adobe was built before 183 as the ranch house of Rancho Aguaje de Centinela and is maintained by the Historica Society of Centinela Valley and Inglewoo City, Dept. of Parks and Recreation. Also or the grounds, the Daniel Freeman Office. The buildings are fine examples of Victorian architecture and furnishings.
HOLLYWOOD PARK Century Blvd. at Prairie Ave. **Inglewood** (213) 678-1181	One of the largest and most beautiful race tracks in the country—the track of lakes and flowers—Hollywood Park provides a de lightful setting where you can watch the fin est of thoroughbred horse racing and harnes racing.
TOWERS OF SIMON RODIA (Watts Towers) 1765 E. 107th St. **Los Angeles** (213) 564-9089	Three unusual towers stand as a monumen to an Italian tile setter, Simon Rodia. For 3 years, he worked single-handedly at his con struction, wiring together steel rods, then stuccoing them with cement and studding the surface with bits of broken china, glass colored tile, shells and old pottery. Today the towers sparkle in the sun, a symbol of man' desire to create his own folk art.

60

Daily
except Sun.

Mon. through Fri.
9 am to 5 pm

Sat. 9 am to 3 pm

Free

Sun. & Wed.
2 pm to 4 pm

Donations accepted

Apr.-July
Thoroughbred racing
post: 2 pm
Aug.-Dec. Harness racing
post: 7:45 pm

Adults: Grandstand $2.25
Clubhouse $4.25
Children under 12 free

Daily
9 am to 5 pm
(later in summer)

Free

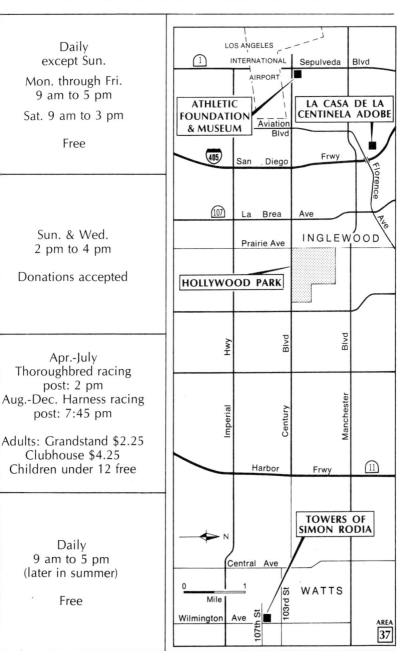

LOS ANGELES
INTERNATIONAL   Sepulveda   Blvd
AIRPORT

**ATHLETIC
FOUNDATION
& MUSEUM**   Aviation
Blvd

**LA CASA DE LA
CENTINELA ADOBE**

405   San   . Diego   Frwy

Florence

107   La   Brea   Ave

Prairie Ave   INGLEWOOD

HOLLYWOOD PARK

Hwy   Blvd   Blvd

Imperial   Century   Manchester

Harbor   Frwy   11

**TOWERS OF
SIMON RODIA**

N

Central Ave

0   1
Mile

WATTS

107th St   103rd St

Wilmington   Ave

AREA
37

LOMITA RAILROAD MUSEUM 250th St. & Woodward Ave. **Lomita** (213) 326-6255	This unique railroad museum is constructed in the style of a Victorian depot, exact in every detail, with hardwood interior and bricked-in yard. Visitors can see a #1765 Mogul built by Baldwin in 1902 and a Union Pacific caboose built in 1910. The museum contains many scale models, photographs and paintings of locomotives.
BANNING MANSION & MUSEUM 401 East M Street **Wilmington** (213) 832-2769	This 1864 carpenters' version of the Greek Revival style of architecture, residence of General Phineas Banning—"father of Los Angeles Harbor," promoter of the railroad and contributor to the development of the West—tells of the history, life styles and decorative arts in California during the 19th century. The house stands in beautiful landscaped grounds.
THE GAMBLE HOUSE 4 Westmoreland Place (off Orange Grove Blvd.) **Pasadena** (213) 793-3334	The house is the most complete and best preserved example of the work of the internationally noted Pasadena architectural firm of Greene and Greene. Built during 1908 the building is a masterpiece of American architecture with hand-shaped heavy beams, broad overhanging eaves, projecting rafter and open sleeping porches. The interiors are carried out in solid teak wood, mahogany, maple and Port Orford cedar, all handrubbed to a glasslike finish.
SAINT SOPHIA CATHEDRAL 1324 S. Normandie **Los Angeles** (213) 737-2424	Seventeen magnificent crystal chandeliers from Czechoslovakia form an imposing part of the very rich and decorative interior of this Greek Orthodox Cathedral. Floors of antique marble, stained glass windows in rare colors and extensive use of pure gold in decoration are outstanding features.

62

Daily, except Mon. & Tues.
10 am to 5 pm

Adults: 50¢
Children: 50¢

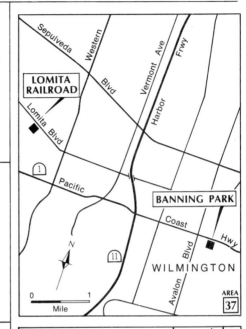

Conducted tours:
Every Wed., Sat. and Sun.
at 1, 2, 3 and 4 pm

Donation requested

Guided tours:
Tues. and Thur.
10 am to 3 pm
and the first Sun.
of each month,
12 noon to 3 pm

Adults: $2.00
Children: free

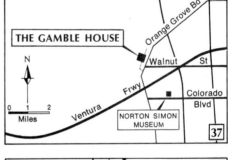

Daily, except Thurs.
9 am to 4 pm

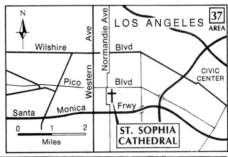

63

DESCANSO GARDENS 1418 Descanso Dr. **La Canada** (213) 790-5571	A magnificent floral showplace covering 16.5 acres, the gardens contain more than 100,000 specimen camelias from China, Japan, England and the southern United States. Myriad rose bushes, orchids, begonias, rhodo dendrons and other plants provide a dazzling display of color throughout the year. There is a charming Japanese garden and Oriental Tea House where tea and cookies are served (closed Mondays).
ROSE BOWL 991 Rosemont Blvd. **Pasadena** (213) 577-4185	Scene of the annual football game played New Year's Day and watched by millions of television viewers, the Rose Bowl is synonymous with the Tournament of Roses, which features each year a two-hour parade of magnificently decorated floral floats. The stadium is open to visitors during the week.
NORTON SIMON MUSEUM Colorado & Orange Grove Blvds. (213) 449-6840	The museum features major exhibitions from the celebrated Norton Simon Foundation collections of old masters paintings, drawings, and tapestries, 19th- and 20th-century paintings and Indian and Southeast Asian sculpture. In the sculpture garden are works by Rodin, Renoir, Maillol and Moore.
CALIFORNIA INSTITUTE OF TECHNOLOGY 1201 East California Blvd. **Pasadena** (213) 795-6811 Ext. 2326	Renowned as one of the world's leading universities in science and engineering, Cal-tech has been a pioneer in the fields of rocketry and space technology. It is also a center for the study of earthquakes, and much of man's knowledge of this subject has been researched here. One-hour walking tours of the campus are offered during regular school semesters.

Daily,
9 am to 5 pm

Free

Daily, except Sat. & Sun.
8 am to 4 pm

Free

Thur., Fr., Sat., Sun.
12 noon to 6 pm

Adults: $1.50
Students with I.D.
and senior citizens: 50¢
Children under 12 free

Tours:
Mon. Thurs. & Fri. 3 pm
Tues. & Wed. 11 am

Free

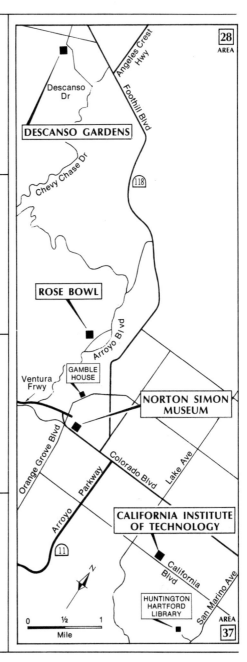

WHAT TO SEE AND WHAT TO DO

MISSION SAN GABRIEL ARCANGEL Mission Dr. at Junipero St. **San Gabriel** (213) 282-5191	Founded on September 8, 1771 by Father Angel Soméra and Pedro Cambon, San Gabriel became the terminus of the long trail from Sonora, Mexico. The mission contains many interesting treasures, artifacts, paintings and rare books. The six bells in the massive tower are approximately 200 years old.
SOUTHWEST MUSEUM 234 Museum Dr. **Los Angeles** (213) 221-2163	Illustrating the history, culture and art of the Southwest Indian, the museum recreates the civilization of the various tribes with displays of their handicrafts and historical relics. Indian portraits and examples of basketry are excellent and the museum's library contains many volumes devoted to archeology.
CASA DE ADOBE 4605 N. Figueroa St. **Los Angeles** (213) 221-2163	Located within walking distance of the Southwest Museum, Casa de Adobe is a replica of a ranch home (hacienda) of the Spanish and Mexican period of early California. Part of the adobe is maintained as a museum and the home is furnished throughout in the style representative of 1800–1850.
LUMMIS EL ALISAL HOME 200 East Ave. 43 **Los Angeles** (213) 222-0546	A 13-room rock structure, built between 1897 and 1910 by the famous Southwestern author, historian, editor, poet and librarian Charles F. Lummis. There is a collection of Indian artifacts in one room and the grounds contain many indigenous flowers and plants. The house is now maintained by the Historical Society of Southern California.

Daily except Mon.
9:30 to 4 pm

Adults: 50¢
Children: 25¢

Daily, except Mon.
1 pm to 4:45 pm

Free

Weds. Sat. and Sun.
1 pm to 4 pm

osed mid-Aug. to mid-Sept.

Free

Daily, except Sat.
1 pm to 4 pm

Free

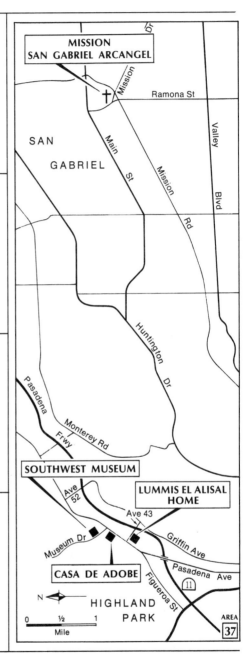

**HUNTINGTON
LIBRARY, ART
GALLERY &
BOTANICAL
GARDENS**

1151 Oxford Road
San Marino

(213) 792-6141

The Huntington consists of three main parts. Within its parklike grounds are a library, with a wealth of manuscripts and rare books in the fields of American and English literature and history; an Art Collection, with a distinguished concentration of British art; and Botanical Gardens, with a dozen specialized gardens of note.

Housing one of the world's finest collections of rare books and manuscripts, the Library is a world-renowned research institution for qualified scholars for the study of British and American history and literature.

On public exhibition in the Library is a copy of the Gutenberg Bible, printed in Mainz about 1450–55, the Ellesmere manuscript of Chaucer's *Canterbury Tales* and other rare books and manuscripts.

In the Art Gallery there are outstanding paintings of the 18th and early-19th centuries by such British artists as Gainsborough, Reynolds, Romney, Turner, Lawrence and Constable. There are also rare tapestries, porcelains, miniatures, sculptures and period furniture pieces.

The Botanical Gardens include shrubs and trees from nearly every continent, and the 12-acre Desert Garden has the largest grouping of cacti and other succulents in the world.

The Huntington has 1,500 varieties of camellias. Their blooming season extends from late fall through April. A history-of-rose walk and a Japanese garden are included in the 130 acres of the Botanical Gardens.

Daily, except Mon.
1 pm to 4:30 pm

Closed during Oct.

Free

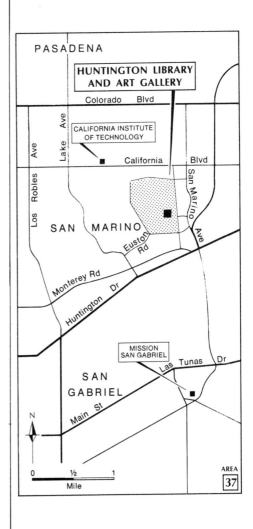

PASADENA

HUNTINGTON LIBRARY
AND ART GALLERY

Colorado   Blvd

Lake   Ave

CALIFORNIA INSTITUTE
OF TECHNOLOGY

Ave

California   Blvd

Los Robles

San Marino

SAN   MARINO

Euston
Rd

Ave

Monterey Rd

Huntington Dr

MISSION
SAN GABRIEL

Las   Tunas   Dr

SAN

GABRIEL

Main   St

N

0   ½   1
Mile

AREA
37

WHAT TO SEE AND WHAT TO DO

LOS ANGELES STATE & COUNTY ARBORETUM 301 N. Baldwin Ave. **Arcadia** (213) 446-8251	127 acres of shrubs, trees, begonias and orchid greenhouses comprise this horticultural research center where a collection of living plants from every continent is grown for educational, research and scientific purposes. Guided tram tours are offered to visitors who may also enjoy seeing some of the historic buildings.
SANTA ANITA PARK 285 W. Huntington Dr. **Arcadia** (213) 447-2171	One of the finest and most famous of thoroughbred horseracing tracks in the country, Santa Anita was the first track to develop and introduce such features as the photo finish, starting gate, electrical timing and the totalizator. Set in the foothills of the San Gabriel mountains. Here you can enjoy horseracing at its very best.
WHITTIER NARROWS NATURE CENTER 1000 North Durfee Ave. **S. El Monte** (213) 444-1872	This 127-acre wildlife and plant sanctuary is situated along the San Gabriel river where several miles of self-guiding nature trails are open to the public daily. Among the lively mixture found in this riverbank community are raccoons, audubon cottontail rabbits, numerous species of migratory ducks, cotton woods, alders, sycamores and many varieties of shrubs.
PIO PICO State Historical Monument 6003 S. Pioneer Blvd. **Whittier** (213) 695-1217	This historic building was the hacienda ranch home of Pio Pico, the last Mexican governor of California. The adobe mansion has been partially restored and contains some original furnishings, providing an interesting look at a typical wealthy household in Mexican California during the nineteenth century.

Daily,
9 am to 5 pm

Free

Autumn racing in Oct.

Winter meeting
Dec. to early April

Adults:
General admission $2.25
Clubhouse $4.00

Children: 17 and under
free with parent

Daily,
9 am to 5 pm

Free

Daily, except Mon. & Tues.
1 pm to 4 pm

House tours:
Adults: 50¢
Children: 6–17 25¢

PACIFICULTURE ASIA MUSEUM 46 North Robles Ave. **Pasadena** (213) 449-2742	Promoting understanding of the cultures of the Pacific and Far East through exhibitions, lectures, music and concerts, the museum is housed in a building of traditional Imperial Palace style, with decorative roof, tiles and stone carvings imported from China. There is a Children's Gallery, Gourmet Gallery, Collector's Gallery where art objects may be purchased, and a museum book store.
MOVIEWORLD 6920 Orangethorpe Ave. **Buena Park** (213) 921-1702	Many cars and planes that have become famous through association with persons or places of historical or theatrical significance are on exhibition in Movieworld. Included in the automotive museum is a 1929 Mercedes-Benz once owned by Al Jolson. In the plane museum are Hitler's super weapons of World War II.
MOVIELAND WAX MUSEUM 7711 Beach Blvd. **Buena Park** (213) 583-8025 (714) 522-1154	Visitors to this reminiscent museum can relive great moments in motion picture history through more than 70 scenes from the cinema and television which are on display. Famous stars of past and present are sculptured in wax. In the Palace of Living Art, masterpieces from the museums of the world are faithfully reproduced in marble, plaster of paris and wax.
CALIFORNIA ALLIGATOR FARM 7671 La Palma **Buena Park** (213) 522-2615	Here is one of the largest and most complete reptile collections in the world. At Alligator Farm you can see great numbers of alligators, crocodiles, snakes, lizards, turtles, tortoises, iguanas, flamingos and many other strange and intriguing creatures. All branches of the reptile family are represented in this unique and exotic collection.

WHEN TO GO AND WHERE TO FIND IT

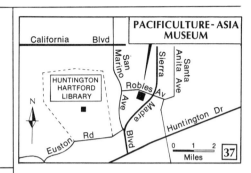

Open: Wed. through Sun.
12 noon to 5 pm

Admission: Adults $1.00

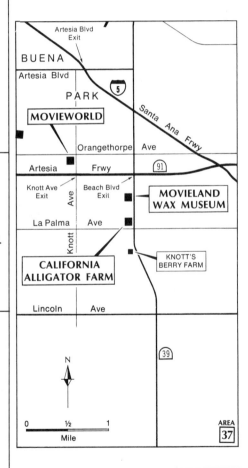

Daily,
Sun. through Thurs.
10 am to 8 pm
Fri. and Sat.
10 am to 9 pm

Adults: $3.50
Children: 5–12 $1.50
Under 5 free

Daily, Jan. 1 to June 10
Sept. 6 to Dec. 31
10 am to 9 pm
June 11 to Sept. 5
9 am to 10 pm
. and Sat. to 11 pm, all year.

Adults: $4.50
Children: 4–11 $2.75
Under 4 free with an adult

Adults: $2.75
Children: 5–14 $1.25
Under 5 free with an adult

WHAT TO SEE AND WHAT TO DO

THE TELEVISION STUDIOS

CBS 7800 Beverly Blvd., **Los Angeles** 90036
NBC 3000 W. Alameda Ave., **Burbank** 91523
ABC 4151 Prospect Ave., **Hollywood** 90027

FOR FREE TICKETS TO SHOWS

The three networks offer visitors an opportunity to be part of a live television audience during the taping of many of their favorite programs. Because of the great demand for tickets, particularly for the more popular shows, application should be made at least one month in advance. Some shows have waiting lists of many months.

All applications should be made in writing, accompanied by a self-addressed, stamped envelope. State the show you wish to see and approximate date you would like to attend.

The envelope should be addressed to the Ticket Division of the studio.

GREEK THEATRE Vermont Canyon Rd. Griffith Park **Hollywood** (213) 666-6000	This beautiful outdoor theatre lies in a natural setting in Griffith Park. Presentations include dramas, ballets and concerts. Programs are changed frequently and visitors should consult newspapers or telephone the ticket office for current attractions and general information.

CONDUCTED
STUDIO TOUR

NBC

Daily, except Sun.
10 am to 5 pm

No reservations. Telephone
845-7000 (ext. 2468)
for further information.

Adults: $2.10
Children: 5–11 $1.40
Under 5 free

Daily,
during summer months

WHAT TO SEE AND WHAT TO DO

**KNOTT'S
BERRY FARM**

8039 Beach Blvd.
Buena Park

(714) 827-1776

Enjoy the "good old days" of the great gold rush of the mid-1800s in the ghost town a Knott's Berry Farm, where accurate recon structions permit you to visit the blacksmith's shop, the general store, the old-time print shop, the gold mine and many more. You can quench your thirst with sarsaparilla in the brass-railed Calico Saloon and strol through the Wells Fargo Office. Board the Butterfield Stage or take a journey on the Ghost Town and Calico Railway, but watch out for masked bandits.

Just outside the ghost town, Fiesta Village brings you the bright color and gaiety o Mexico; you can buy souvenirs from south o the border and enjoy real Mexican food from the Cantina.

Relive the twenties at Knott's new Roaring 20's Area and Airfield. Here are seven excit ing thrill rides, including the Corkscrew loop coaster, the 20-story drop on the Sky Jump, plus the Whirlwind, Loop Trainer Flying Machine and the Motorcycle Chase. Take a spin on the Gasoline Alley, Knott's Bear-y Tales ride or the Sky Cabin. Attractions such as the Palms Casino/Buffalo Nickel Penny Arcade and the Pilot's Rec Area invite guests to old-fashioned 1920s games.

Nearby stands a magnificent full-scale rep lica of Independence Hall, where young guides dressed in the fashion of the late 1700s will guide you on an absorbing tour.

On Knott's Lagoon visitors can travel into the old South aboard the majestic Cordelia K as the white side-wheeler brings back the days when steamboats plied the great Mississippi.

Daily entertainment during the summer in the 2,150-seat Good Time Theatre, plus five other stages, free with the price of admission.

Forty shops offer tourists everything from high-button shoes to the latest fashions. For dining you can visit the Chicken Dinner Res taurant, the Steak House or one of the many snack bars.

Daily,

Winter:
10 am to 6 pm
Mon., Tues. and Fri.

Closed Weds. and Thurs.

Sat. 10 am to 10 pm
Sun. 10 am to 9 pm

Summer:
9 am to midnight

General admission:
Adults: $4.25
Children: 3–11 $2.75
Under 3 free

TUCKER WILDLIFE SANCTUARY Star Route to Modjeska Canyon, **Orange** (714) 649-2760	This unusual wildlife sanctuary is famous fo the many hummingbirds that inhabit the area throughout the year. These and many othe species may be viewed from a special obser vation porch and patio. A naturalist is or duty to aid in identification. There are numerous nature trails and a small museum with interesting exhibits.
BRIGGS CUNNINGHAM AUTOMOTIVE MUSEUM 250 East Baker St. **Costa Mesa** (714) 546-7660	An outstanding collection of antique, classic sports racing and racing cars. Featuring a 1927 Bugatti "Royale," Duesenbergs and others, all maintained in running condition. The museum art collection contains origi nal works by leading automotive artists in the U.S.A. and abroad.
MOVIELAND OF THE AIR Orange County Airport **Santa Ana** (714) 545-1193	A $2.5 million collection of famous aero planes featured in motion pictures and televi sion is displayed in studio-style sets. Authen tic WW I & II fighting planes, Jenny trainer, early mail planes and many others, plus weapons and arms displays, models and engines make this one of the finest collec tions of aeronautical memorabilia in the world.
CHARLES W. BOWERS MEMORIAL MUSEUM 2002 N. Main St. **Santa Ana** (714) 834-4024	Exhibits of science, history and art are pre sented in this museum, which contains many fine Indian and early California relics, furni ture paintings, clothing and weapons. The exhibits in the three galleries are changed frequently.

Daily,
9 am to 4 pm

Adults: 50¢
Children: 50¢

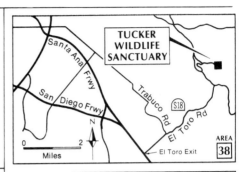

Daily, except Mon. and Tues.
9 am to 5 pm

Adults: $2.50
Students, Military with I.D.
$1.50
Children: 5–12 50¢
Under 5 free

Daily:
10 am to 5 pm
Closed Mon. during winter

Adults: $2.25
Children: 12–17 75¢
5–11 50¢
Under 5 free

Daily, except Mon.

Tues. through Sat.
9 am to 5 pm

Weds. & Thur.
7 pm to 10 pm

Sun. 1 pm to 5 pm

Free

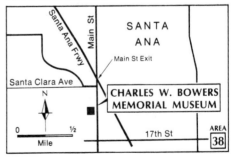

DISNEYLAND

1313
Harbor Blvd.
Anaheim

(714) 533-4456

Disneyland is a delight for all ages and an experience that can be enjoyed again and again.

Divided into sections, each with its own unique charm and appeal, Disneyland offers the visitor an exploration of the Old West in *Frontierland;* the world of fantasy, Peter Pan, Dumbo, and Alice in Wonderland in *Fantasyland;* crocodiles, hippopotamuses and other fearsome creatures on a river trip in *Adventureland,* and a scientifically authentic, simulated trip to the moon plus experiences of other futuristic wonders in *Tomorrowland,* including the thrilling new adventure through outer space "Space Mountain."

The 1850s of New Orleans is recreated in *New Orleans Square.* From the square, an exciting boat ride, "Pirates of the Caribbean", will take you through the midst of a fierce pirate battle. Boat trips on the stern-wheeler *Mark Twain* and the 1790 sailing ship *Columbia* present a fascinating contrast to an underwater voyage in one of the eight "atomic" submarines where mermaids, sea serpents and pirates' treasure may be seen. The Matterhorn's thrilling bobsled ride, the Haunted Mansion and other attractions abound.

The entire Disneyland area is served by nine specially designed trains, including a monorail system. There are numerous restaurants, snack bars and coffee shops, and, while you should come prepared for much walking and wear comfortable shoes, there are many seats where you can rest for a while. Strollers are available for young children.

General admission:

Adults: $5.50

Children: 12–17 $4.50
3–11 $2.50
Under 3 free

Mid-June to Mid-Sept.
Daily: 8 am to 1 am

Rest of year:
10 am to 6 pm
Wed. through Fri.
9 am to 7 pm Sat. & Sun.

Closed Mon. & Tues.

Open daily during
Christmas and Easter
vacation periods.

Note: these hours
are subject to change.

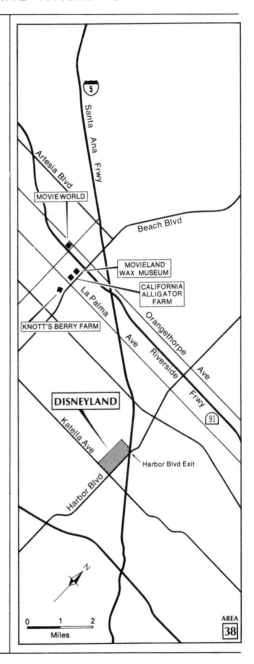

81

WHAT TO SEE AND WHAT TO DO

PALOS VERDES ART CENTER & MUSEUM 5504 W. Crestridge Road, **Rancho Palos Verdes** (213) 541-2479	The Art Center is the home of the Palos Verdes Community Art Association where members may participate in a wide variety of arts and crafts, including painting, print making, etching and work in stone, wood and clay. There is an Art Rental and Sales Gallery and frequent exhibitions of work by some of the West's foremost artists and craftsmen.
RANCHO SANTA ANA BOTANIC GARDENS 1500 North College Ave. **Claremont** (714) 626-3922	An outstanding collection of native California plants and flowers covers 83 acres, set against a magnificent backdrop of the San Gabriel Mountains. The main blooming period in the garden is from late February to the middle of June. Particularly striking are the plantings of manzanitas, California lilacs, fremontias, tree poppies and bush anemones.
ADOBE de PALOMARES 491 East Arrow Highway **Pomona** (714) 620-2300	Built between 1850 and 1854, the Adobe de Palomares stands today as a fine example of the Spanish rancho era. Authentically restored to its original form and appearance—with the exception of the interior of the north wing which housed the kitchen, dining room and storeroom—the adobe is furnished in the style of the period.
ARABIAN HORSE SHOWS Kellogg Campus California State Polytechnic Univ. 3801 West Temple **Pomona** (714) 598-4153	Many of the nation's finest purebred Arabian horses are bred at the Kellogg Campus where horse shows are presented on Sunday afternoons during the months of October, November and January through May. Visitors will see demonstrations of jumping, cattle penning, side-saddle, driving, liberty horse, dressage, etc. Many trophies and ribbons of the past are on display.

Museum:
Tues. through Fri.
10 am to 4 pm

Sat. 11 am to 2 pm
Sun. 1 pm to 4 pm

Free

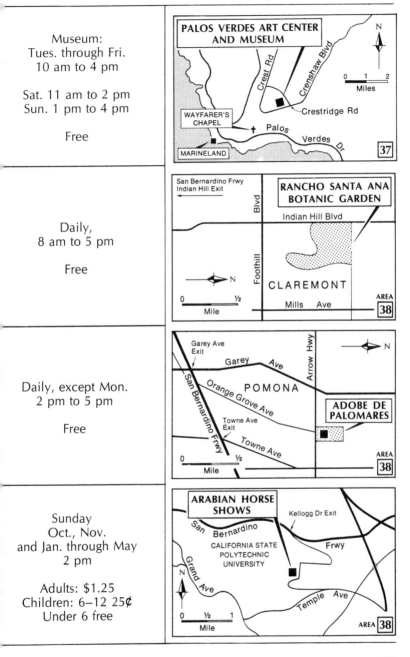

PALOS VERDES ART CENTER AND MUSEUM

Crest Rd

Crenshaw Blvd

N

0 1 2
Miles

Crestridge Rd

WAYFARER'S CHAPEL

Palos

Verdes Dr

MARINELAND

37

Daily,
8 am to 5 pm

Free

RANCHO SANTA ANA BOTANIC GARDEN

San Bernardino Frwy
Indian Hill Exit

Blvd

Indian Hill Blvd

Foothill

N

CLAREMONT

0   ½
Mile

Mills   Ave

AREA 38

Daily, except Mon.
2 pm to 5 pm

Free

Garey Ave Exit

Garey   Ave

Arrow Hwy

N

San Bernardino Frwy

Orange Grove Ave

POMONA

Towne Ave Exit

Towne Ave

ADOBE DE PALOMARES

0   ½
Mile

AREA 38

Sunday
Oct., Nov.
and Jan. through May
2 pm

Adults: $1.25
Children: 6–12 25¢
Under 6 free

ARABIAN HORSE SHOWS

Kellogg Dr Exit

San Bernardino

CALIFORNIA STATE POLYTECHNIC UNIVERSITY

Frwy

Grand Ave

N

Temple Ave

0   ½   1
Mile

AREA 38

WINTER SPORTS AREAS

Owing to the very large number of locations and the variety of facilities available, winter skiing resorts are not listed in this guide. The California Chamber of Commerce issues an excellent free Winter Sports Guide, covering the entire state. General skiing information may also be obtained from the Far West Ski Association (in Los Angeles telephone (213) 483-8551, in San Francisco (415) 781-2535.

SCENIC CHAIR RIDES
Summer months only

Some of the major winter ski centers open their facilities during the summer. Visitors may enjoy a spectacular and unusual ride on a ski chair life to the top of a mountain to see magnificent views of the surrounding country.

It should be noted that, in general, the chair lifts are in operation on weekends and holidays only. As times and days of operation vary, a telephone call is advisable before starting your journey.

Four of the ski centers which will be operating their chair lifts during the summer are:

HOLIDAY HILL
SKI LIFTS
Wrightwood

(714) 249-3256

SNOW
SUMMIT
Big Bear Lake

(714) 866-4621

MT. BALDY
Mt. Baldy

(714) 982-4208

GOLDMINE
Moonridge

(714) 585-2517

HOLIDAY HILL SKI LIFTS

Adults $2.00
Children: 5–12 $1.00
Under 5 free

MT. BALDY

Adults: $4.00
Children: 6–12 $3.00
Under 6 free

GOLDMINE

Adults: $2.00
Children: Under 13 $1.00

SNOW SUMMIT

Adults: $2.00
Children: 12–16 $1.50
3–11 $1.00
Under 3 free

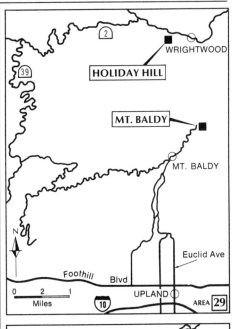

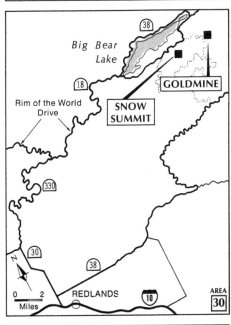

85

BURTON'S TROPICO GOLD MINE, MILL & MUSEUM Mojave Tropico Rd. **Rosamond** (805) 256-2648	The mine and mill are kept in the same condition they were when gold mining was a flourishing industry, so visitors may tour them and learn how gold and silver were extracted from the ore. On the grounds is the main mine shaft, 900 feet deep. The museum contains historical artifacts and mining equipment. Conducted tours of mine and mill.
PIERCE COLLEGE Nature Center and Farm 6201 Winnetka Ave. **Woodland Hills** (213) 884-4455	Four interesting tours are given at the college. They cover the Life Science Museum, Nature Center, Farm and Braille study of nature. Each lasts from 1½ to 2 hours. The Farm tour includes views of pigs, chickens, sheep, horses, dairy cattle and other domestic animals.
BEULAH HAWKINS DOLL MUSEUM 1437 Sixth St. **Santa Monica** (213) 394-2981	Over 3,000 collectors' items are featured in this doll museum, ranging in value from $5 to $3,000 each. The exhibits include a 150-year-old animated English doll house, a Japanese Samurai doll and a collection of French fashion dolls. The museum occupies nine rooms of an old mansion built in the late 1800s.
J. PAUL GETTY MUSEUM 17985 Pacific Coast Highway **Malibu** (213) 459-2306	The J. Paul Getty Museum building re-creates the splendor of a 1st-century Roman villa, the Villa dei Papiri. Three major collections—Western European Paintings, Greek and Roman Antiquities and French Decorative Arts—are displayed in 38 galleries. There is also a collection of over 100,000 photographs in the Photo Archives.

WHEN TO GO AND WHERE TO FIND IT

Daily,
Mine: Closed Tues. & Wed.
Goldcamp: Oct. 1 to June 1
weekends only 10 am to 4 pm

Tours: Gold Mine
Adults: $3.50
Children: 5–11 $1.50
Comb. tickets available

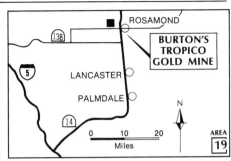

Conducted tours
Mon. through Sat.
By reservation only
(one week notice required)

Free

Daily:
Mon. through Sat.
1 pm to 5 pm
Sun. by appointment

Adults: $2.00
Children: 12–17 $1.00
Under 2 free

Daily,

Mon. through Fri.
June through Sept.

Tues. through Sat.
Oct. through May

10 am to 5 pm
Free

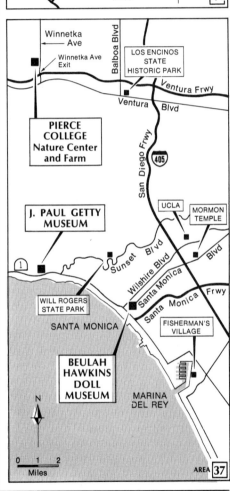

WHAT TO SEE AND WHAT TO DO

DEATH VALLEY NATIONAL MONUMENT

Park Headquarters
are located at
Furnace Creek

(714) 786-2331

This great valley—a desert lying to the east of the Sierra Nevada range—takes its name and its reputation from the winter of 1849 when a group of pioneers, seeking a short-cut to the goldfields, became trapped in its barren wasteland. It was here, also, that the 20-mule teams hauled borax from the desert mines and where "Death Valley Scotty" built his famous castle.

The best months to visit Death Valley are between November and late April. During the summer months temperatures frequently reach 120° F. and can go as high as 134° F. It is strongly recommended that you call first at the Monument Headquarters and Visitor Center at Furnace Creek to pick up a leaflet giving hints on safe driving in the desert. Leaflets are available listing numerous places of interest—ghost towns, Scotty's Castle, Harmony Borax Works, Ubehebe Crater, Zabriskie Point and others.

Note: *The Park Service warns that there is extreme congestion of roads and campgrounds in Death Valley every year at the following times: three day weekends during the winter season, Death Valley '49ers encampment, 1st or 2nd week in November, Thanksgiving weekend, Christmas-New Year's week and Easter week. For your own enjoyment it is suggested that you avoid these dates if possible.*

AMARGOSA OPERA HOUSE

Death Valley Junction
(714-Death Valley Junction No. 8)

A unique program of ballet-pantomimes has been created by Marta Becket, whose performances at the Opera House are frequently a memorable experience. Her creation of many characters—humorous, sad, comical and tragic—is carefully blended into a program the whole family can enjoy. During peak periods of the winter season it is advisable to make reservations for seats well in advance.

88

WHEN TO GO AND WHERE TO FIND IT

All year

Free

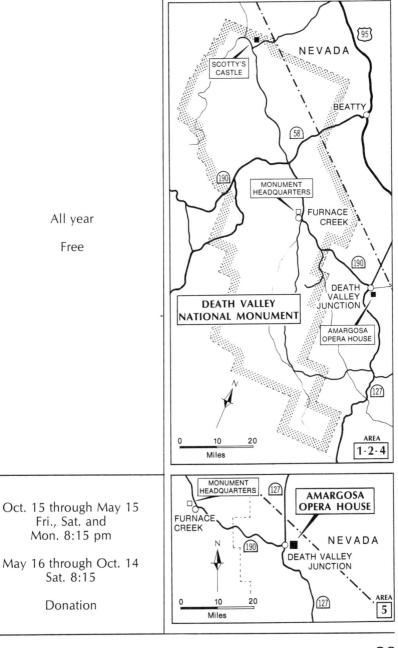

Oct. 15 through May 15
Fri., Sat. and
Mon. 8:15 pm

May 16 through Oct. 14
Sat. 8:15

Donation

89

SCOTTY'S CASTLE

North End of
Death Valley

(714) 786-2331
(Monument
Headquarters)

Scotty's Castle is an amazing sight in this desolate region. A combination of Moorish, Spanish, Italian and California Mission architecture, it was built many years ago at the whim of the late "Death Valley Scotty," a wealthy and eccentric personality.

Furnished with luxurious rugs, tapestries and elaborately carved furniture, it fully reflects Scotty's flamboyant and expensive tastes. The Castle is owned and operated by the National Park Service and is part of the Death Valley National Monument. Daily tours of the interior are held throughout the year. A gift shop and small snack bar are open to visitors.

Note: *The Park Service warns that there is extreme congestion of roads and campgrounds in Death Valley every year at the following times: three day weekends during the winter season, Death Valley '49ers encampment, 1st or 2nd week in November, Thanksgiving weekend, Christmas-New Year's week and Easter week. For your own enjoyment it is suggested that you avoid these dates if possible.*

DESERT MUSEUM

Butte Ave.
Randsburg

(714) 374–5891

Established by the Desert Lions Club as an archive for the fabulous Rand Mining District, the museum contains many mining artifacts, photographs and equipment relating to the days when Randsburg was a lively boom town.

In 1895 gold was discovered at the Yellow Aster Mine above the present site of the town. The mine yielded an estimated $25 million.

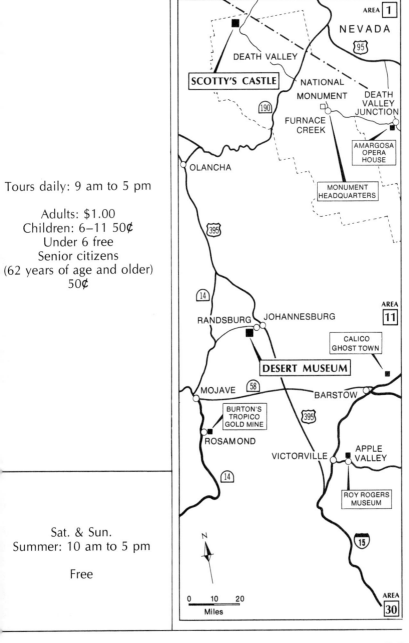

Tours daily: 9 am to 5 pm

Adults: $1.00
Children: 6–11 50¢
Under 6 free
Senior citizens
(62 years of age and older)
50¢

Sat. & Sun.
Summer: 10 am to 5 pm

Free

PROVIDENCE MOUNTAINS STATE RECREATION AREA Essex	Formerly Mitchell Cavern State Reserve, this 5,280-acre area is situated on the eastern slope of the Providence Mountains. The park headquarters adjoin Mitchell Caverns, great subterranean chambers and passageways formed some 12 million years ago. The El Pakiva and Tecopa Caverns are open to the public. They are dry, well lit and have stairs and railings to facilitate guided tours.
JOSHUA TREE NATIONAL MONUMENT Nearest town: **Twentynine Palms**	Bearing its cream-white blossoms, the picturesque Joshua Tree dominates this desert, located in beautiful high country. The monument was created in order to preserve this area where, in Spring, wild flowers lay color across the sands and the tall Mojave juccas, cactus and spiny ocotillo share the land with the desert animals.
CALICO GHOST TOWN Regional Parks **Yermo** (714) 254-2122	A silver mine town that enjoyed peak prosperity during the late 1800s and is now a famous Ghost Town comes to life again. Relax for a few hours in the past as you walk through the streets. Visit the general store, bottle house, the old school house, Boot Hill, a pottery works and other attractions. Explore Maggie Mine, one of the most famous silver mines in Western history.
ROY ROGERS DALE EVANS MUSEUM 15650 Seneca Road, **Victorville** (714) 234-4548	Mementos of the personal and public lives of Roy Rogers and Dale Evans may be seen in this interesting museum which houses a large collection of pictures, trophies and mounted animals. Roy's famous horse, Trigger, is included among the exhibits.

Daily, 8 am to 5 pm
Tour Center may be
closed at any time
due to bad weather or
work in the area.

Closed July, Aug. and Sept.)

Adults: 50¢
Children: 6–17 25¢
Under 6 free

All year
Monument headquarters
Daily, 8 am to 5 pm

Free

Daily,
9 am to 5 pm

$1.00 per car
Campground $3.00
per night per unit

Daily,
9 am to 5 pm

Adults: $1.50
Juniors: $1.00
Children: 50¢
Under 6 free

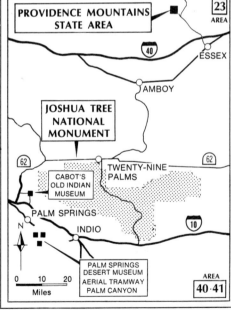

PALM SPRINGS AERIAL TRAMWAY **Palm Springs** (714) 325-1391	Two 80-passenger cable cars carry travelers safely and smoothly in a spectacular ride from the valley station to the mountain terminal lodge located at the 8,516 foot level of Mt. San Jacinto State Park. There are snack and cocktail bars and a gift shop at the valley station, while at the mountain lodge station there are gift and apparel shops, an Alpine Restaurant and a cocktail bar. A free 25-minute color motion picture, "Miracle of Palm Springs," is shown at the mountain station every hour. At the top of the tramway there are 54 miles of hiking trails and in winter months there is a snow play area where toboggans and snow saucers may be rented for fun on the slopes.
PALM CANYON Agua Caliente Indian Res. Palm Canyon Drive **Palm Springs**	Palm Canyon forms part of the valley which was the traditional summer retreat for the Agua Caliente Indians. Magnificent stands of native California Fan Palms can be seen here and in the adjoining tributary canyons—Andreas, Murray and Fern. There are still traces of old Indian campsites where mortar holes, gouged in large rocks, were once used for grinding meal.
PALM SPRINGS DESERT MUSEUM 101 Museum Drive, **Palm Springs** (714) 325-7186	A cultural and educational museum devoted to art, the natural sciences and the performing arts. The Science Wing features permanent exhibits of the desert's natural sciences, Indians of the South west, as well as the changing science exhibits. The Art Wing features changing exhibits in the fine arts, primitive and folk art.

Daily,
10 am to 9 pm

Adults: $4.50
Children: 12 - 17 $3.50
4 - 11 $2.00
Under 4 free

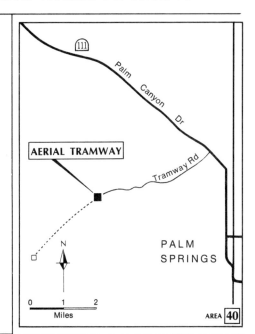

Daily,
9 am to 4:15 pm
Oct. 1 to May 30

Closed June to Oct.

Adults: $1.00
Children: 6–12 25¢
Under 6 free

Late Sept. through June

Tues. through Sat.
10 am to 5 pm
Sun. 2 pm to 5 pm
Closed Mon.

Adults: $1.50
ree first Tues. of each month)
Children and students: free

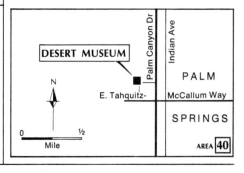

95

CABOT'S OLD INDIAN PUEBLO MUSEUM 67-616 E. Desert View Ave. **Desert Hot Springs** (714) 329-7610	This 35-room Hopi structure was built by Cabot Yerxa over a period of 20 years, using only his hands, the earth and cast-off material. Since his death in 1965 the monument has been preserved and kept open to the public. The museum contains Indian artifacts, beadwork and other early 20th century Indian and Eskimo tools and materials. There is also an art gallery and a trading post.
PALOMAR OBSERVATORY **Palomar Mountain** (213) 795-6811 (Public Rel.)	The 200-inch Hale telescope in the Palomar Observatory is the largest in this hemisphere, actually a giant camera with which astronomers take pictures of objects up to one billion light years away. The visitors' gallery in the dome of the Hale telescope and the exhibit hall are open to the public.
SAN JACINTO MUSEUM 181 East Main St. **San Jacinto** (714) 654-4952	Natural history exhibits and displays of local geology and paleontology are featured in this museum which records the history of the area over a wide span, from the aboriginal Indians to the early American settlers.
EDWARD-DEAN MUSEUM OF DECORATIVE ARTS 9401 Oak Glen Rd. **Cherry Valley** (714) 845-2626	A spacious eight-room museum situated in the midst of 16 beautifully landscaped acres offers a wide variety of outstanding European decorative art—furniture, paintings, tapestries and porcelains. In addition there is sculpture dating from the 3rd Century B.C. and an important selection of Oriental pieces. Changing exhibition programs feature outstanding work by contemporary artists.

96

Daily, except Tues.
9:30 am to 5 pm

Guided tours only

Adults: $1.00
Children: 5–16 50¢
Under 5 free

Daily,
9 am to 5:30 pm

Free

Daily, except Mon.
1 pm to 5 pm

Free

Tues. through Sat.
10 am to 5 pm
Sun. 1 pm to 5 pm
Closed Mon.

Free

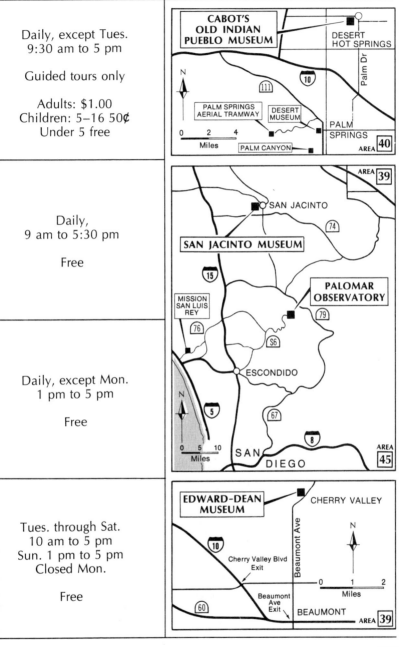

LINCOLN SHRINE Smiley Park at 4th & Eureka Sts. **Redlands** (714) 793-6622	Photographs, art, books and curios are on display in this museum covering the life of President Lincoln. Many personal effects and hand-written documents, including those of other dignitaries of the period, are shown. The library contains over 3,000 volumes on the Civil War and Lincoln, and dozens of manuscripts written by leading Civil War personalities.
SAN BERNARDINO ASISTENCIA 26930 Barton Rd. **Redlands** (714) 793-5402	Built by the Franciscan Fathers in 1830–34, the Asistencia was a branch of the San Gabriel mission and was intended to form a unit in an inland chain then under discussion by authorities in California. The Asistencia fell into ruin in the late 1860s but has since been well restored. It contains two museums and a wedding chapel.
MISSION INN 3649 7th St. **Riverside** (714) 784-0300	Constructed in mission style, this famous and historic inn contains many interesting collections of paintings, antiques and artifacts. Over 700 bells are on display, a large collection of international dolls and many Spanish paintings. The St. Francis Chapel contains a 200 year old altar from Guanajuato, Mexico.
ORANGE EMPIRE RAILWAY MUSEUM 2201 South A St. **Perris** (714) 657-2605	Equipment and mementos from the era of electric railroading are on display in this unusual museum. Among the multitude of rail vehicles are steam cars, electric freight equipment and work and construction cars once used by interurban and street railways. Visitors may ride on the streetcars and other equipment, which is manned by specially trained volunteer motormen and conductors.

Daily, except Sun. & Mon.
1 pm to 5 pm

Free

Daily, except Mon.
Wed. through Sat.
10 am to 5 pm

Tues. and Sun.
1 pm to 5 pm

Free

Daily,
11:30 am to 2:30 pm

Adults: $1.50
Children: 6–12 50¢
Under 6 free

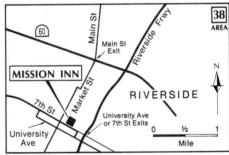

Daily, 9:30 am to 5:30 pm

Cars operate on
Sat., Sun. and holidays

Museum: free

Rides:
Adults: $1.00
Children: 5–12 50¢
Under 5 free

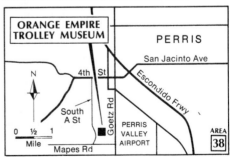

99

GRIFFITH PARK

Park Ranger
Headquarters
4730 Crystal
Springs Dr.
Los Angeles

(213) 665-5188

Covering 4,252 acres, this very large and fin
city park contains the Los Angeles Zoc
Greek Theatre, Ferndell Museum, Trave
Town, and observatory and planetarium
bird sanctuaries, nature trails, 18 large picni
areas, tennis courts, ball diamonds and sce
nic drives. The major attractions are liste
individually in this guide.

A free map of Griffith Park detailing i
many miles of hiking and bridle trails can b
obtained from the Headquarters, or from th
Public Relations Office, Room 1350, Ci
Hall East, Los Angeles 90012. Telephon
485-5555. For information about Griffit
Park's five golf courses call: 661-8524 c
485-5572.

**LOS ANGELES
ZOO &
CHILDREN'S
ZOO**

5333
Zoo Drive
Los Angeles

More than 3,300 mammals, birds and rep
tiles can be seen in the 80 acres of exhib
areas.

The Zoo is divided into five continenta
areas with the animals shown in small repli
cas of their native habitat. The aviary has
central flight cage which visitors may wal
through. Polar bears, seals, sea lions an
other aquatic animals enjoy the large pool i
their compound while 700 specimens c
snakes and lizards slither around in the Rep
tile House.

The Children's Zoo is a delight to all mem
bers of the family. Here the gentler animal
are on display and many may be petted an
fed. Happy Hollow is extremely popular wit
city children who are enchanted by the expe
rience of petting and feeding gentle barnyarc
animals such as lambs, goats, chickens and
geese.

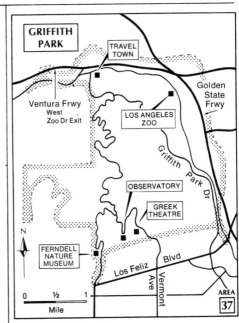

All Year

Ranger Headquarters
Daily, 9 am to 5:30 pm

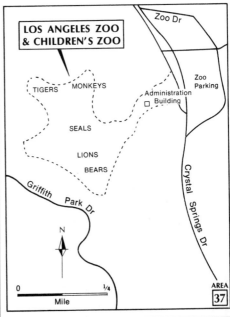

Daily,
Summer: 10 am to 6 pm
Winter: 10 am to 5 pm

Adults: $1.50
Children: 12–15 75¢
Under 12 free with adult
Senior citizens free

101

GRIFFITH OBSERVATORY, PLANETARIUM AND HALL OF SCIENCE

Located in **Griffith Park** at the north end of Vermont Ave.

(213) 664-1191

An outstanding feature of the observatory is the planetarium theatre where days, years and even centuries can be compressed into minutes so that the sun, moon, planets and stars can be shown in their proper places at any time in the past or in the future. Other special effects are used to create eclipses, sunsets, northern lights and journeys into space.

The observatory regularly produces planetarium programs on various topics. The programs last about an hour. CHILDREN UNDER 5 ARE ADMITTED ONLY TO THE FIRST SATURDAY SHOW.

The twin refracting telescope may be used by visitors every evening (weather permitting) from dusk until 10 pm. (7 pm to 10 pm in winter).

The Hall of Science features astronomical displays and exhibits of physical scientific achievements.

FERNDELL NATURE MUSEUM

5375 Red Oak Drive **Griffith Park**

(213) 467-1661

This small museum contains many nature and botanical exhibits. Fresh indoor displays of plants and flowers in season are shown each with descriptive information.

A regular program of films on nature, travel and outdoor recreation is shown each week at the Ferndell Ranger Station.

Times vary:
Telephone 664-1191
for current information

Adults: $1.50
Children: 13–17 $1.00
5–12 50¢

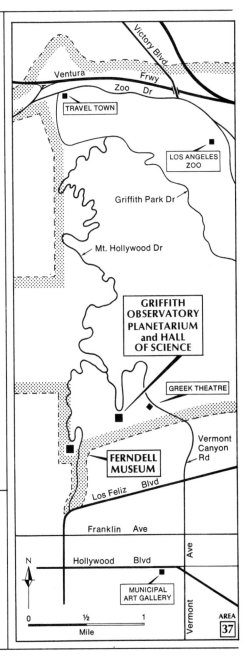

Wed. through Sun.
1 pm to 5 pm
Telephone 467-1661 for
film program information

Free

TRAVEL TOWN in Griffith Park 4730 Crystal Springs Dr. **Los Angeles** (213) 662-5874	An extensive collection of different modes of transportation is on display. Youngsters and adults can examine, walk through and sit in airplanes, cable cars, fire engines and trains of a bygone era. Trolley rides, available on an original Los Angeles trolley, are very popular with young visitors.
LOS ANGELES CITY HALL 200 N. Spring St. **Los Angeles**	Four hundred fifty-four feet high, the City Hall is located in the Civic Center in downtown Los Angeles. The Rotunda Art Gallery is on the third floor and the Observation Tower on the twenty-seventh floor affords a fine panoramic view of the city.
CHINATOWN 900 N. Broadway and vicinity **Los Angeles**	Pagoda-styled buildings, shops and restaurants form a sharp Asian contrast to the rest of Los Angeles. Pungent smells of Oriental cooking blend with incense from the small stores where gourmets can purchase dried shark's skin, lotus root, fish and other delicacies.
LITTLE TOKYO First St. Central, Second and Main (area) **Los Angeles**	Gift shops, restaurants, book stores and markets are to be found in this busy Japanese-American community. Cultural studios teach Japanese dancing, flower arranging, painting and other arts. During August the Nisei Festival Week is held in Little Tokyo.

WHEN TO GO AND WHERE TO FIND IT

Daily,
9 am to 5:30 pm

Museum free

Trolley rides
Adults: 35¢
Children: 25¢

Daily,
10 am to 4 pm
Mon. through Thur.
10 am to 10 pm Fri.
11 am to 5 pm Sat. & Sun.

Free

All year

All year

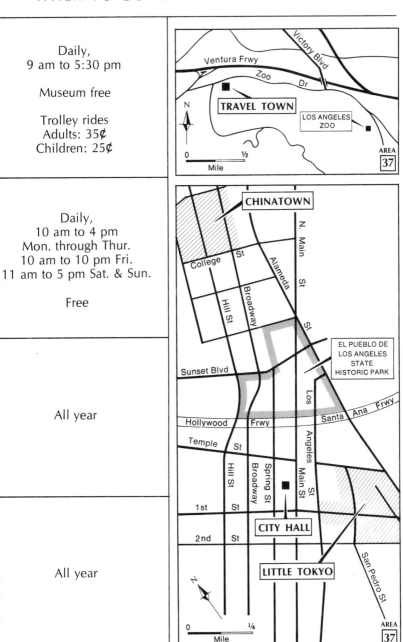

WHAT TO SEE AND WHAT TO DO

EXPOSITION PARK Bounded by Exposition, Figueroa, Santa Barbara and Menlo Sts. **Los Angeles**	This civic cultural and recreational center i set around a seven-acre sunken garden con taining 15,000 rose bushes. It contains the museums of Science and Industry and of Nat ural History; the Memorial Coliseum, home of the USC and UCLA collegiate and pro Rams football teams, the Memorial Sport Arena and the Swim Stadium.
CALIFORNIA MUSEUM OF SCIENCE AND INDUSTRY 700 State Dr. Exposition Park **Los Angeles** (213) 749-0101	An outstanding museum encompassing the fields of energy, mathematics, communica tions, space, agriculture and industry. Visi tors can operate push-button exhibits; the many displays are sure to delight children o all ages. The Hall of Health dramatizes human physiology and has extensive information on narcotics.
L.A. COUNTY MUSEUM OF NATURAL HISTORY 900 Exposition Blvd. **Los Angeles** (213) 746-0410	Four major halls of animals of the world in natural habitats; Hall of Cenozoic Mammals; dinosaurs; insects; birds; Pre-Columbian artifacts; South Pacific Ethnology; Indians; American History from 1660 to 1814 and from 1860 to 1914; minerals; Marine Hall. Free films each Sat. at 2 pm. Free concerts each Sun. at 2 pm. Note: Museum located in Exposition Park.
UNIVERSITY OF SOUTHERN CALIFORNIA Special events, Alumni House University Park **Los Angeles** (213) 741-2983	The University is the oldest major private coeducational establishment in the west and occupies a campus of 150 acres, with 81 permanent buildings. The grounds are attrac tively landscaped and particularly beautiful in the spring and summer when the magnolia trees are in bloom. Conducted walking tours of the campus are given by USC students.

106

WHEN TO GO AND WHERE TO FIND IT

All year

Free

Daily,
10 am to 5 pm

Free

Daily, except Mon.
10 am to 5 pm

Free

Conducted tours (one hour)

Mon. through Fri.
10 am to 2 pm

By appointment:
call (213) 741-2983

Free

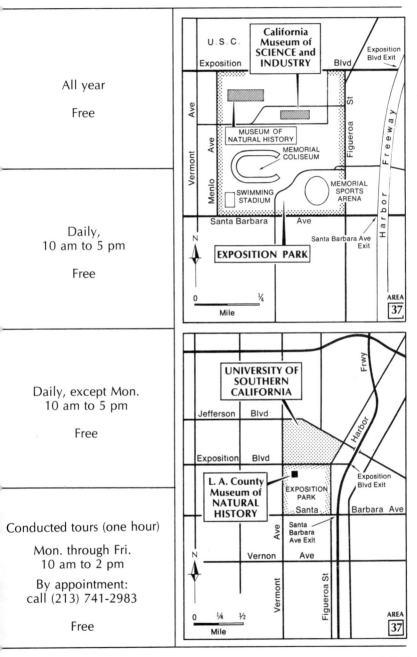

LOS ANGELES PUBLIC LIBRARY 630 West 5th Street **Los Angeles** (213) 626-7461	An outstanding California reference room will be found in this civic library, the largest west of the Mississippi. In addition to the many specialized departments, visitors will see numerous sculptures, murals and frescoes created by artists of the Public Works Art Project.
MUSIC CENTER FOR THE PERFORMING ARTS First St. at Grand Ave. **Los Angeles 90012** (213) 626-7211	The Dorothy Chandler Pavilion is the home of the Los Angeles Philharmonic Orchestra. Its presentations range from ballet to symphony and opera. The Ahmanson Theater offers musical comedy and drama while the Mark Taper Forum features chamber music, drama and other performing arts. For information on current programs, consult newspapers or telephone the ticket office.
OCCIDENTAL CENTER 12th St. at Hill & Olive **Los Angeles** (213) 748-8111	Home of the Occidental Life Insurance Company, Occidental Center is a 32-story commercial office complex containing authentic Japanese gardens, a garden court, fountains and pools. There is also a fine auditorium. At the top of the building is a restaurant which offers diners magnificent views across the city. The observation deck, also open to the public, is 400 feet above the street.
EL PUEBLO DE LOS ANGELES State Historic Park Main St. and Sunset Blvd. **Los Angeles** Visitor center (213) 628-7164	This historic area contains a number of restored buildings which formed part of the social and commercial heart of Los Angeles during its very early years. Guided walking tours are offered Tues. through Sat. 10 am to 2 pm (June, July and August), 10 am to 12 noon during the remainder of the year. Tours start at the Pueblo Commission Visitor Center, 100 Plaza Plaza St.

108

Daily, except Sun.
10 am to 9 pm

Free

Tours:
Mon. through Fri.

Tel. 626-7211 (ext. 366)
for times and information.

Daily,
except Sat. and Sun.
Observation deck
10 am to 11 am
2 pm to 4 pm

Free

Free

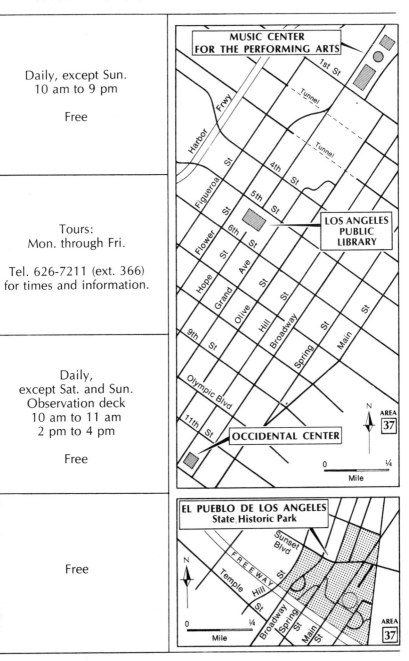

Historic landmarks to be visited include:

OLD MISSION CHURCH
(Nuestra Senora la Reina de Los Angeles)
N. Main St. and Sunset Blvd.

Founded by the Franciscans in 1814, the church is still in service and is the oldest religious edifice in the city.

OLD PLAZA FIREHOUSE
134 Plaza St.

An original horse-drawn pumper, chemical wagon and other early Fire Department memorabilia can be seen in this restored building, constructed in 1884 to house Volunteer Engine Company No. 1.

OLD SPANISH PLAZA
N. Main St. and Sunset Blvd.

In Spanish days, the Plaza was the center of activity for the whole town. Just to the north of the plaza is **Olvera Street,** the oldest street in the city. Paved in red brick and tile, it stands as a replica of an old Mexican village where sidewalk booths and shops sell pottery, jewelry and other handicraft products. Restaurants offer good Mexican food. The evenings are colorful and gay as Mexican music from the cafes fills the air.

PICO HOUSE
500 N. Main St.

The first major hotel and social center of Los Angeles. It was build by Pio Pico, the last Mexican Governor of California, in 1870.

Daily

Free

Mon. through Fri.
10 am to 3 pm

Sat. and Sun.
11 am to 5 pm

Free

Shops open daily from about
10 am to 10 pm

During summer,
some shops remain open
to midnight

Can only be seen
by guided tour.

Tues. through Sat.
10 am to 1 pm

Free

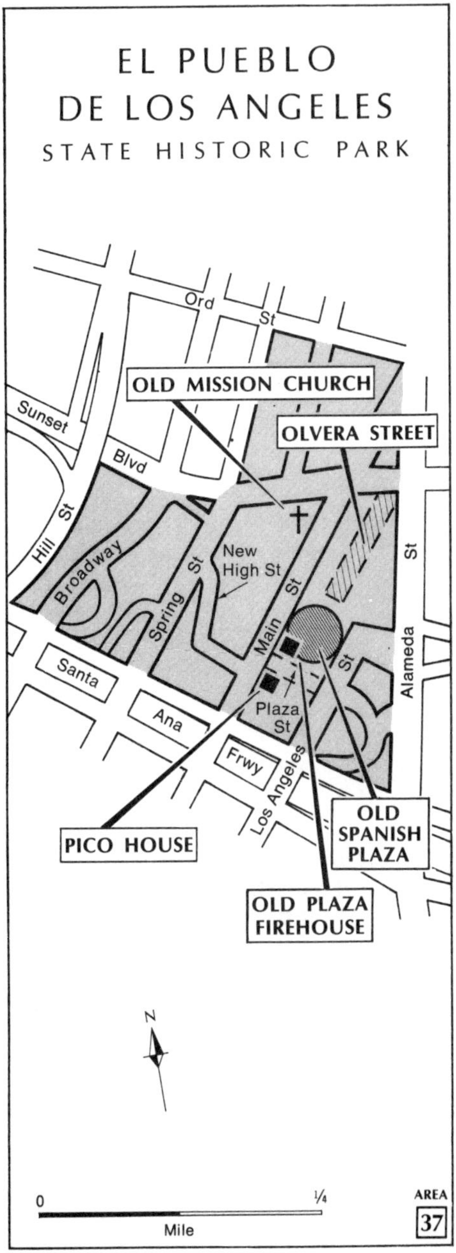

EL PUEBLO DE LOS ANGELES
STATE HISTORIC PARK

Ord St

OLD MISSION CHURCH

OLVERA STREET

Sunset

Blvd

Hill St

Broadway

Spring St

New High St

Main St

Santa

Ana

Plaza St

Frwy

Los Angeles

Alameda St

PICO HOUSE

OLD SPANISH PLAZA

OLD PLAZA FIREHOUSE

N

0   ¼
Mile

AREA
37

111

BROOKSIDE VINEYARD COMPANY Assumption Abbey Winery 9900 A St. **Guasti** (714) 983-2787	Brookside Vineyard Company has been operated by members of the same family for more than 140 years. At the Guasti winery are primary aging cellars, blending and bottling facilities, laboratories and a Wine Museum. It also reportedly has the largest underground aging cellar in the United States. Visitors are invited to roam the winery and its tasting rooms.
THOMAS VINEYARDS 8916 Foothill Blvd. **Cucamonga** (714) 987-1612	Thomas Vineyards date back to 1839 when Tiburcio Tapia was given the Cucamonga land grant by Juan Alvarado, governor of Mexico. Tapia built an adobe home, planted a vineyard and started one of California's first wineries. Relics and equipment of earlier days are on display in the sales room and on the grounds. Visitors are welcome to tour the winery and learn about the art of winemaking.
BEAR MOUNTAIN WINERY Di Giorgio Rd. **Bakersfield** (805) 845-2231	The Bear Mountain Winery of the M. LaMont Company welcomes visitors to its vineyards on the western slope of Bear Mountain, where varietal grapes for premium blends of table wines are grown. The tasting room is open every day and conducted tours of the winery permit visitors to learn about the art of winemaking.

Daily,
9 am to 3:30 pm
(self-guided tours)

Sat. & Sun. 11 am to 4 pm
(conducted tours on the hour)

Free

Daily,
8 am to 6 pm

Self-guided tours

Free

Daily:
12:30 pm to 3:30 pm

Conducted tours

Free

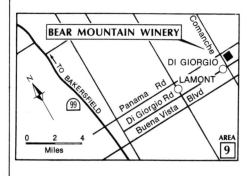

113

COMPANY	BUSINESS
AIRSTREAM 15939 Piuma Ave. Cerritos	Travel trailers
CAPITOL RECORDS 1750 Vine St. Hollywood	Recording
GENERAL MOTORS 2700 Tweedy Blvd. South Gate	Automobile assembly
GOODWILL INDUSTRIES 342 San Fernando Road Los Angeles	Renovation of useful articles by handicapped people
VAN NUYS AIRPORT 6950 Hayvenhurst Av. Van Nuys	Airport operations
LOS ANGELES FIRE DEPARTMENT covering the Greater Los Angeles area	Public service
LOS ANGELES INTERNATIONAL AIRPORT 1 World Way Los Angeles	Airport operations
LOS ANGELES TIMES Times Mirror Sq. Los Angeles	Newspaper publication

TELEPHONE	CHILDREN	GENERAL INFORMATION
213) 860-4411 Ext. 228	Yes	Mon. through Fri. 10 am and 2 pm. 1½-hour tours
(213) 462-6252	Yes	Tues. and Thurs. 6 pm Tours last approx. 1 hour
(213) 566-4141 Ext. 214	Min. age 9	Mon. through Fri. 11:30 am and 6:30 pm Tours last 1 hour
(213) 223-1211	Yes	Mon. through Fri. 10 am to 3 pm Not suitable for very young children. Tours last 1 hour
(213) 873-1383	Min. age 6	Mon. through Sat. By reservation
Check local listing	Yes	Visitors welcome to tour any fire station during normal daylight working
(213) 646-5740	Min. age 6	Mon. through Sat. 9:30 am and 10:45 am Tours last 1 hour
(213) 625-2345 Ext. 1218	Min. age 10	Tues. and Fri. 2:45 pm Tours last 1 hour

COMPANY	BUSINESS
DUNCAN CERAMICS PRODUCTS, INC. 5673 E. Shields Ave. Near Clovis (Fresno)	Ceramics
FRIANT DAM CANALS AND TROUT HATCHERY Friant	Trout Hatchery
PACIFIC STOCK EXCHANGE 618 S. Spring St. Los Angeles	Investment transactions
PACIFIC TELEPHONE 420 S. Grand Ave. Los Angeles	Telephone operations
LOBUE BROTHERS INC. 201 Sweetbriar Lindsay	Citrus packing
DEPARTMENT OF WATER & POWER 111 N. Hope St. Los Angeles	Utilities
WESTERN AIRLINES 6060 Avion Dr. Off Century Blvd. Los Angeles	Airline operations
U.C.L.A. CENTER FOR HEALTH SCIENCES 10833 Le Conte Blvd. Los Angeles	Teaching, research

TELEPHONE	CHILDREN	GENERAL INFORMATION
(209) 291-4444	Yes	Wed. and Thurs. 9 am to 12 noon 1 pm to 2:30 pm by appointment
(209) 487-5113	Yes	Daily, 9 am to 5:30 pm
(213) 489-4800	Yes	Mon. through Fri. 8:30 am to 12:30 pm Tours last 25 minutes
(213) 621-1779	Min. age 18	Mon. through Fri. 9:30 am to 7:30 pm Tours last 1½ hours
(209) 562-2548	Yes	Mon. to Fri. 9 am to 4 pm mid-Nov. through Aug.
(213) 481-6343	Yes	Mon. through Fri. 8 am to 3:30 pm Tours last 1 hour
(213) 646-2345	Min. age 13	Mon., Wed. & Sat. 9 am to 3 pm Wed. evening 7 pm to 9 pm
Volunteer office (213) 825-6001	Min. age 16	Mon. through Thurs. 10 am to 12 noon. Tours last 2 hours

COMPANY	BUSINESS
GENERAL MOTORS ASSEMBLY 8000 Van Nuys Blvd. Van Nuys	Automobile assembly
INDEPENDENT PRESS-TELEGRAM 604 Pine Ave. Long Beach	Newspaper publication
PROCTER & GAMBLE MANUFACTURING CO. 1601 W. Seventh St. Long Beach	Soap, detergents and food products
PETER PAUL INC. 1800 South Abbott St. Salinas	Candy
THE DAILY BREEZE 5215 Torrance Blvd. Torrance	Newspaper publication
MCCORMICK & CO., INC. 1311 Schilling Place Salinas	Spices
NUTRILITE PRODUCTS, INC. 5600 Beach Blvd. Buena Park	Manufacturing food supplements and cosmetics
ORANGE COUNTY COURTHOUSE 700 Civic Center Dr. W. Santa Ana	Municipal and Superior Courts

TELEPHONE	CHILDREN	GENERAL INFORMATION
(213) 997-5153	Yes	Mon. through Fri. 12:15 pm Tours last 1 hour
(213) 435-1161 Public Service Dept.	Yes	Mon. through Fri. 10 am and 2 pm Tours last 1 hour
(213) 432-6981 Ext. 203	Min. age 13	Tues. and Thurs. 2 pm Wed. 1:30 pm Tour and 15-minute film
(408) 424-0481	Min. age 8	Tues. and Thurs. at 10 am. Closed first 3 weeks in July
(213) 540-5511 Ext. 282	Min. age 10	Mon., Thurs. and Fri. 9 am to 3:45 pm Tours last 1 hour
(408) 758-2411	Yes	Tues. and Thurs. at 1 pm by appointment
(714) 521-3900 Ext. 211	Yes	Mon. through Thurs. 9:30 am or 12:30 pm Tours last 1½ hours
(714) 834-2303	Min. age 10	Mon. through Fri. 9 am to 3 pm Tours last 2½ hours

COMPANY	BUSINESS
LOS ANGELES TIMES 1375 Sunflower Ave. Costa Mesa	Newspaper publication
STEWART ORCHIDS, INC. 1212 East Las Tunas Dr. San Gabriel	Blooming orchids Best time to visit is between mid-Feb. and mid-May.
SAN BERNARDINO CENTRAL FIRE STATION 456 N. Mount View San Bernardino	Public service
DYNAIR ELECTRONICS, INC. 5275 Market Street, San Diego	Television equipment and electronics
HUMPHREY, INC. 9212 Balboa Ave. San Diego	Manufacturing precision instruments
KFMB-TV-CHANNEL 8 7677 Engineer Road, San Diego	Television and broadcasting
SHIELDS DATE GARDENS 80-225 Highway 111 Indio	Date and citrus cultivation
LEMON PACKING HOUSE OF THE GOLETA LEMON ASSN. 100 La Patera Lane Goleta	Lemon packing

120

TELEPHONE	CHILDREN	GENERAL INFORMATION
(714) 540-5151	Min. age 10	Mon. through Fri. by appointment Tours last 1 hour
(213) 287-8974	Min. age 9	Tours last 1 hour Tour days and time by appointment
(714) 383-5286	Yes	Visitors welcome to tour the fire station facilities during normal daylight working hours
(714) 263-7711	Min. age 12	Mon. through Fri. 9 am to 11 am 2 pm to 3 pm Tours last 1 hour
(714) 565-6631	Min. age 9	Mon. through Fri. 10 am to 3 pm Tours last 30 minutes
(714) 292-5362	Min. age 10	Tues. and Thurs. mornings by appointment Tour lasts 1 hour
(714) 347-0996	Yes	Visitors are welcome. Daily, 8 am to 6 pm
(805) 967-2355	Min. age 10	Mon. through Fri. 8 am to 3 pm Tours last 1 hour

TRAVEL NOTES

INDEX

ABC Television Studios **74**
Adobe Chapel **12**
Adobe de Palomares **82**
Aerospace Museum **4**
Alpine Village **62**
Amargosa Opera House **88**
Arabian Horse Shows **82**

Banning Mansion and Museum **62**
Bazaar de Mundo **12**
Bear Mountain Winery **112**
Beulah Hawkins Doll Museum **86**
B. F. Goodrich Co. **114**
Botanic Gardens, Santa Barbara **38**
Botanical Building, San Diego **4**
Briggs Cunningham Automotive Museum **78**
Brookside Vineyard **112**
Burton's Tropico Gold Mine **86**
Busch Bird Sanctuary **52**

Cabot's Old Indian Pueblo Museum **96**
Cabrillo Marine Museum **28**
Cabrillo National Monument **14**
Calico Ghost Town **92**
California Alligator Farm **72**
California Institute of Technology **64**
California Museum of Science & Industry **106**
California Oil Museum **42**

Capitol Records **114**
Casa de Adobe **66**
Casa de Estudillo **10**
Casa de Lopez **10**
Catalina Island **46**
Catalina Terminals, Inc. **46**
CBS Television Studios **74**
Channel Islands National Monument **42**
Charles W. Bowers Memorial Museum **78**
Children's Zoo, Los Angeles **100**
Children's Zoo, San Diego **2**
Chinatown **104**
Citizens Savings Athletic Museum **60**
City Hall, Los Angeles **104**
Coliseum **106**
County Museum of Art, Los Angeles **56**
County Museum of Natural History, Los Angeles **106**

Daily Breeze **118**
Death Valley National Monument **88**
Department of Water & Power, Los Angeles **116**
Derby Pendleton House **12**
Descanso Gardens **64**
Desert Museum **90**
Disneyland **80**
Dos Pueblos Orchid Co. **38**
Dynair Electronics, Inc. **120**

125

Edward Dean Museum of
  Decorative Arts **96**
El Dorado Nature Center **24**
El Presidio Real de San Diego **14**
El Pueblo de Los Angeles State
  Park **108**
Exposition Park **106**

Farmers Market **56**
Ferndell Nature Museum **102**
Fine Arts Gallery **4**
Fisherman's Village, Marina del
  Rey **32**
Fisherman's Wharf, Redondo
  Beach **32**
Forest Lawn Memorial Park,
  Glendale **54**
Forest Lawn Memorial Park,
  Hollywood Hills **52**
Fort Tejon State Historic Park **48**
Fowler Museum **56**

Gamble House **62**
General Motors, Southgate **114**
General Motors, Van Nuys **118**
Getty Museum **86**
Glass-Bottom Boat Trip **46**
Goldmine Scenic Chair Rides **84**
Goodwill Industries **114**
Grauman's Chinese Theater **54**
Greek Theatre **74**
Griffith Observatory &
  Planetarium **102**
Griffith Park **100**

Hall of Champions **4**
Hall of Science **102**
Harbor Excursions, San Diego
  16
Hearst San Simeon State
  Historical Monument Park **44**
Historical Society Museum, Santa
  Barbara **36**
Holiday Hill Scenic Chair Rides
  84
Hollywood Bowl **52**

Hollywood Park **60**
Hollywood Wax Museum **54**
House of Pacific Relations **6**
Humphrey, Inc. **120**
Huntington Library & Art
  Gallery **68**

Independent Press-Telegram,
  Long Beach **118**
Irvine Bowl **22**

J. Paul Getty Museum **86**
Joshua Tree National Monument
  92

Kern County Museum & Pioneer
  Village **48**
KFMB-TV-Channel 8, San Diego
  120
Knott's Berry Farm **76**

La Brea Tar Pits **56**
La Casa de la Centinela Adobe
  60
La Casa de Rancho Los Cerritos
  26
Laguna Beach Museum of Art **22**
La Jolla Caves **20**
La Jolla Museum of
  Contemporary Art **20**
La Purisima Mission State Historic
  Park **40**
Lawry's California Center **48**
Lemon Packing House of the
  Goleta Lemon Assoc. **120**
Leonis Adobe **50**
Lincoln Shrine **98**
Lion Country Safari **24**
Little Tokyo **104**
Living Sea **26**
Lomita Railroad Museum **62**
Long Beach, Catalina Cruises **46**
Long Beach Museum of Art **28**
Los Angeles Children's Zoo **100**
Los Angeles City Hall **104**
Los Angeles Civic Center **104**

126

Los Angeles County Museum
106
Los Angeles County Museum of
Art **56**
Los Angeles Fire Department
114
Los Angeles International
Airport **114**
Los Angeles Memorial Sports
Arena **106**
Los Angeles Mormon Temple **58**
Los Angeles Municipal Art
Gallery **54**
Los Angeles Public Library **108**
Los Angeles State & County
Arboretum **70**
Los Angeles Swimming Stadium
106
Los Angeles Zoo **100**
Los Encinos State Historic Park
50
Los Angeles Times, Orange
County Edition **120**
Los Angeles Times **114**
Lummis El Alisal Home **66**

Magic Mountain **50**
Marineland of the Pacific **30**
Marineland Sky Tower **30**
Maritime Museum Association,
San Diego **16**
Mayfair Music Hall **32**
Mission San Diego de Alcala **18**
Mission Inn, Riverside **98**
Mission La Purisima **40**
Mission San Buenaventura **34**
Mission San Fernando Rey de
Espana **50**
Mission San Gabriel Arcangel
66
Mission San Juan Capistrano **22**
Mission San Luis Obispo de
Tulosa **40**
Mission San Luis Rey de Francia
18
Mission San Miguel Arcangel **42**

Mission Santa Barbara **34**
Mission Santa Ines **40**
Mormon Temple **58**
Morro Bay Aquarium **42**
Mount Baldy Scenic Chair Rides
84
Movieland of the Air **78**
Movieland Wax Museum **72**
Movieworld **72**
Museum of American Treasures
18
Museum of Art, Los Angeles **56**
Museum of Art, Santa Barbara
36
Museum of Man **6**
Museum of Natural History, Los
Angeles **106**
Museum of Natural History, San
Diego **6**
Museum of Natural History, Santa
Barbara **38**
Museum of Science & Industry,
Los Angeles **106**
Music Center for the Performing
Arts **108**

Natural History Museum, San
Diego **6**
Natural History Museum, Santa
Barbara **38**
Navy Open House **14**
Naval Training Center Museum
14
NBC Television Studios **74**
Norton Simon Museum **64**
Nutrilite Products, Inc. **118**

Occidental Center **108**
Old Globe Theatre **6**
Old Mission Church **110**
Old Plaza Fire House **110**
Old San Diego **10**
Old Spanish Plaza **110**
Old Town Drug Store **12**
Old Town San Diego **10**
Olvera Street **110**

127

Orange County Courthouse **118**
Orange Empire Trolley Museum **98**

Pacific Coast Stock Exchange **116**
Pacific Telephone **116**
Pacificulture-Asia Museum **34**
Palm Canyon **94**
Palm Springs Aerial Tramway **94**
Palm Springs Desert Museum **94**
Palomar Observatory **96**
Palos Verdes Art Center and Museum **82**
Pasadena Rose Bowl **64**
Paul Getty Museum **86**
Pendleton House **12**
Pico House **110**
Pierce College Nature Center & Farm **86**
Pio Pico State Historic Monument **70**
Ports O'Call Village & Whaler's Wharf **28**
Procter & Gamble Manufacturing Co. **118**
Providence Mountains State Area **92**
Public Library, Los Angeles **108**

Quail Botanic Gardens **18**
Queen Mary **26**

Rancho Los Alamitos **28**
Rancho La Brea Tar Pits, George C. Page Museum **56**
Rancho Santa Ana Botanic Gardens **82**
Reuben H. Fleet Space Center **2**
Rose Bowl **64**
Roy Rogers Museum **92**

Salk Institution **20**
San Bernardino Asistencia **98**
San Bernardino Fire Department **120**

San Buenaventura Mission **34**
San Diego Botanical Building **4**
San Diego Children's Zoo **2**
San Diego Fine Arts Gallery **4**
San Diego Harbor Excursions **16**
San Diego Mission **18**
San Diego Museum of Natural History **6**
San Diego Union Office **10**
San Diego Wild Animal Park **8**
San Diego Zoological Gardens **2**
San Fernando Rey Mission **50**
San Gabriel Mission **66**
San Jacinto Museum **96**
San Juan Capistrano Mission **22**
San Luis Obispo County Historical Museum **40**
San Luis Obispo Mission **40**
San Luis Rey Mission **18**
San Miguel Mission **42**
San Onofre Nuclear Information Center **22**
San Simeon **44**
Santa Anita Park **70**
Santa Barbara Botanic Garden **38**
Santa Barbara County Courthouse **36**
Santa Barbara Historical Society Museum **36**
Santa Barbara Mission **34**
Santa Barbara Museum of Art **36**
Santa Barbara Museum of Natural History **38**
Santa Barbara Zoological Gardens **36**
Santa Catalina Island **46**
Santa Ines Mission **40**
Scenic Chair Rides **84**
Scenic Terrace Drive **46**
Scotty's Castle **90**
Scripps Institution of Oceanography **20**
Seabee Museum **34**
Seal Rookery Boat Trip **46**
Sea World **16**

128

Serra Museum Library & Tower
    Art Gallery **14**
Shields Date Gardens **120**
Skyline Drive **46**
Snow Summit Scenic Chair
    Rides **84**
Southern California Gas Co. **116**
Solvang **38**
South Coast Botanic Gardens **32**
Southwest Museum **66**
Space Theater & Science Center
    2
Spanish Village Arts & Crafts
    Center **8**
Stewart Orchids, Inc. **120**
St. Sophia Cathedral **62**

Television Studios **74**
Thomas Vineyards **112**
Timken Art Gallery **8**
Towers of Simon Rodia **60**
Travel Town **104**
Tucker Wildlife Sanctuary **78**

UCLA Botanical Gardens **58**
UCLA Center for Health
    Sciences **116**
UCLA Frederick S. Wight Art
    Galleries **58**
Universal Studios Tour **52**
University of California, Los
    Angeles **58**
University of Southern
    California **106**

Ventura County Historical
    Museum **34**

Watt's Towers **60**
Wayfarers Chapel **30**
Western Airlines **116**
Whaley House **12**
Whittier Narrows Nature Center
    70
Wild Animal Park **8**
William S. Hart Park **48**
Will Rogers State Park **58**
Wineries **112**

129